The Whole Classroom Left Behind

The Whole Classroom Left Behind

Observations From A Failing Inner City School

James W. Shine

Copyright © 2015 James W. Shine
All rights reserved.

ISBN: 1511542764
ISBN 13: 9781511542760
Library of Congress Control Number: 2015905415

CreateSpace Independent Publishing Platform, North Charleston, South Carolina

Dedicated to: All of the Good Kids stuck in Bad Schools through
NO FAULT OF THEIR OWN.

Table of Contents

Foreword · ix

Chapter 1   Background · 1
Chapter 2   Welcome To The Jungle · 3
Chapter 3   Good Teachers · 13
Chapter 4   The Not So Good Teachers · 20
Chapter 5   Noise And Chaos · 25
Chapter 6   M&M · 29
Chapter 7   Kevin And Friends · 32
Chapter 8   How They Saw Me · 36
Chapter 9   The Mechanics Of The Place · 38
Chapter 10 Why They Are The Way They Are · · · · · · · · · · · · · · · · 47
Chapter 11 Maybe This Is Why They Are The Way They Are · · · · · · · · · · · 55
Chapter 12 Glimmers Of Hope · 60
Chapter 13 What My City Is Doing · 69
Chapter 14 What My State And Our Nation Are Doing · · · · · · · · 86
Chapter 15 What More Can Be Done · 101
Chapter 16 What You Can Do For Your Child · · · · · · · · · · · · · · · 129

Epilogue · 154

Foreword

In the pages of first hand observations that follow, I have purposely not named the large northeastern inner-city school system that I still work in presently as a paraprofessional. Partly this is in fear of retribution against myself- whistle-blowers have, we all know, often been chastised. But, more importantly, I don't feel that my impoverished hometown's school system isn't really any worse (or better) than most of the others across the nation and therefore shouldn't be singled out. After all, every public school in the nation has suffered the traumatic damages done from the implementation of the "No Child Left Behind Act" (2001) and the "Individuals With Disabilities Education Act" (2004) recently put into effect. These damages are certainly unintended, as these acts were undoubtedly well meaning, but the woes they have produced have severely impacted our school systems, and form much of the backdrop for what you will read in the pages that follow. In keeping with this, I have changed the name of the inner-city middle school where I work as well as the names of my fellow paraprofessionals and teachers (as well as the students mentioned) to protect their privacy. But remember everything you will be reading is true, and strange as these vignettes may seem; actually happened!

1
Background

I had tried everything to make a living. I was a college graduate, but I was an older man now. I was sixty years old, short, fat and white and the world had kind of left me behind. In earlier years I had worked at almost everything, I had driven a truck and had worked in retail; I had been a social worker for the State of Connecticut placing geriatric patients in convalescent and nursing homes and had investigated reports of neglect and child abuse. I had been the State of Connecticut's official auctioneer auctioning the State's surplus vehicles in Wethersfield for eight years. That had been a lot of fun.

I had done many private auctions and fund-raising auctions for charity but little by little my auction career had come to an end. I think that this was in large measure due to the fact that EBAY was developed and most people began to use that as the preferred auction method.

I had been a financial advisor, well actually more a discount stockbroker. What I would do is basically help elderly Portuguese and Italian men place stock trades. These guys were more gamblers than investors and since they didn't know how to use computers I could make commissions just placing their unsolicited transactions.

All day long I'd scream into my rotary 'phone "Buy one hundred shares of this" or "Sell one hundred shares of that" and so the pleasant time went by and I even got paid at the end of the month! I had a little storefront office downtown and there was a lot of excitement on a daily basis as my little coterie of "investors" would keep me company, watching the computer screen with me; cheering and groaning as the stocks and options that they had bet on gyrated up and down. Unfortunately as the years went along these uncomputer literate elderly men slowly passed away, and as the Internet established itself big-time and more and more people began to use it for their speculative investments, fewer and fewer customers needed me anymore causing "bingo securities", as I derisively used to privately call my business, to go belly up!

Basically I had been left behind technologically, I had never keep up with computers so one field after another closed up for me. So I found myself, as I said at sixty years old with my unemployment checks running out, and my younger wife kept saying to me; "I've got to work so you gotta work", "I've gotta work so you gotta work"! So I was forced to continue looking for a job. I sent resumes out by the hundreds but responses were slow in coming and for whatever reason (possibly age discrimination?) I was invited to very few employment interviews. Finally, on a lark, I decided to send a resume to my local northeastern city school system. Now my large Connecticut city where I had been living for thirty-six years, and where I had raised my family, has a population of over 110,000 people and had never been known to have a good public school system.

I lived in the farthest outer suburbs of this city but I was well aware that at the time that I applied 21 out of it's 29 schools were considered "failing" under the federal No Child Left Behind Act. I sent in an application as a paraprofessional, basically a teacher's aide, and this was the beginning of quite an adventure!

2
Welcome to the Jungle

In the fall of 2008 I took the test for paraprofessional and found it unbelievably easy.

After scoring near the top of the group and being sent for a urine test, a fingerprinting session and jumping through other bureaucratic hurdles I was eventually offered a paraprofessional position by the city. I started in January 2009 at an inner-city middle school; we'll call it "Williams Middle School", which comprised children of sixth, seventh and eighth grades. There were approximately 1500 students at this school subdivided into three "houses" of 500 students apiece each named for one of the assistant principals. Prominently displayed near the glass front doors was a big sign that said: "Home of the Lions". Later on I would learn that was the name of the school's basketball team. Not much later than that I would come to wish that the sign could be changed to read: "Home of the Little Monsters"!

As I reported to work on first day of school right after Xmas vacation what a cacophony of sounds assailed my ears as I entered the main hallway! Teachers were screaming at the top of their voices; "Lockers, lockers. People, people" it was enough to wake the dead. Students were screaming back to the teachers and to one another just as loudly. The names of the children were unbelievable to me. Because I was sixty years old and I hadn't been in a school in thirty or forty years and I had come from a time when children's names were "Richard" and "George" and "Mary" I was quite unprepared when I heard: "Moesha, Roesha, Myesha, Tyquan, Myquan, to your lockers! To your lockers! Quick, quick! People, people!" The teachers sounded like drill sergeants at a Marine

Corp. boot camp. Lockers slammed as students rushed to make it to their first classes.

My new students were a colorful bunch; kind of "Pirates of the Caribbean" like. Many of them sported tattoos, earrings and lots of baubles and bling. To me, at least, a very very strange looking group. Eighty percent of them were black or Hispanic. I was soon assigned to various classrooms and set to work doing my new job.

Due to the strangeness of my young charges' names I found remembering them difficult. I often wondered why parents would give children these names. I had always had a pretty good memory but these modern kids names really threw me for a loop.

Why, for example, would a parent call their son "Femi"? Is that a good name for a boy? It seems like this would create problems throughout life. But so it was, there were children named "Femi". The teachers explained to me when I questioned about the weirdness of the kids names that these students and their families had come from forty or fifty different countries and all sorts of nationalities and racial backgrounds were being reflected. The ages of my students should have been 12 to 14 but many of them had stayed back numerous times and some of them were as old as 17 and 18. In the hallways Spanish was spoken by the kids as commonly as English. Well, actually, English wasn't much spoken by them either. Instead an ebonic black, "ghetto speak" better reflected the dialect of the black students in the hallways and classrooms. Many of the white students of the inner city spoke the same way as their black fellow students and used the exact same lingo. Day after day I would hear: "I axed you dis" or "I axed you dat" and even the teachers were so used to that sort of thing that I never heard a teacher correct it.

Ninety percent of the children qualified for free or reduced price lunches and Williams Middle School was officially designated by the federal "No Child Left Behind Act" as a failing school. In the hallways Mongoloid students giggled and laughed as they went from class to class. As they were very friendly children, sometimes they would even come up and hug me. The catchment area for our school was one of our city's low-income areas and the feeder elementary schools for Williams were also all failing schools with bad reputations for disciplinary problems and wild behavior. As a matter of fact, while I was working for the city, one of these feeder schools had made the national news as the principal had forbidden XMAS celebrations on school property. Some of my fellow paraprofessionals pushed children around in wheelchairs many of whom were incontinent and didn't seem to have much of a clue as to where they were going. They were pushed around the hallway from class to class and many of my co-workers ribbed me because I wasn't relegated to diaper duty as they were. Remember I hadn't spent much time in the public schools since the 1960s so I was shocked to see all these disabled kids with all the individualized attention and manpower needed to take care of them. When I questioned the teachers as to why my new home differed so much from the schools of my youth it was explained to me that everything that I saw had resulted from the changes mandated by the "No Child Left Behind Act" of 2001 and the "Individuals With Disabilities Education Act" of 2004. These acts had filled up the schools with children who in previous times, for example when I was younger, might have gone to some type of specialized institution or would have been educated utilizing a home-schooling arrangement.

Not wanting to be considered an "old fogey" I went along with all these changes that had happened in the schools during my thirty or forty year absence and tried to be good natured and good humored about the new practices that I was observing. But on my first day when I was assigned to my first individualized attention student, we'll call him "Jose"; I was stunned to find out how low his cognitive abilities were. As I sat beside him in the classroom, trying to get him to write a few words, he would constantly scream "Mr. Shine, Mr. Shine, I'm tired, I'm tired"! Then I'd say: "Jose, you've only written your name and as a matter of fact only half of your name, not even your last name."

"I'm tired, I'm tired", he'd shout in response, turning red in the face. Then he would put his head down on the desk and rest. This would happen day after day. Constantly he would holler out in the middle of class, "I've got to go, go to the toilet, I have to do brown, brown!!" The teachers would scream for him to be quiet (as he usually shouted this ten times a class period even when he had just returned from the bathroom) and would look at me as if it was my job, somehow or other, to keep him silent. Talking with the teachers, who were mostly young women aged 25 through 35, and who mostly had a good relationship with the students and did a remarkable job, I was told that many of these kids were the unfortunate victims of fetal alcohol syndrome. As a result of this and similar problems caused by the fact that their mothers often abused drugs as well while pregnant with these children, they now they had difficulties remembering even the simplest facts that the teachers were trying to impart. They, and many of the kids that I, as a special education para was assigned to work with, had as much difficulty retaining information as my eighty-three year old mother-in-law had. And she had Alzheimer's!

Jose, with his slightly misshapen head and his spindly, almost stick-like, arms and legs together with his shuffling uncoordinated gait was probably a pretty good example of what they were talking about. Now Jose was basically a good kid and a good hearted one at that. Sometimes, when he wasn't having one of his tantrums, he could be kind and giving to his fellow students but, nevertheless, any class period that was unlucky enough to have him in it was a period that was going to be interrupted at least half a dozen times driving even the most patient teacher to despair. Yes, young teenagers like Jose, 13, 14 and 15 years old were unable to remember hardly anything that they were taught. Of course they didn't try very hard! Jose spelt farm "frm", he spelt made "mde". He often even misspelled his own last name! Unfortunately there were many "Joses" among my caseload. But in addition to these children's cognitive disabilities the worst part was their behavior. They were constantly jumping up and down in class, interrupting the teacher in mid-sentence, and causing general disruption throughout the classroom.

For years I had thought that teachers had a cushy job, quite a nice deal. But I soon came to realize that a teacher's life was very, very difficult in the inner-city school I had just joined. As I said before, almost all of them were young women in their late 20's or early 30's and, by and large, they did the best that could be expected given the obstacles that they had to work with. The biggest problem was that they had to spend 70-80% of their time during each period on classroom management leaving only a small fraction of time available for actual teaching! Many classrooms were regularly in chaos. Special Ed students, and many mainstream kids who were often even more disruptive, threw monkey wrenches into the teacher's lesson plans. Kids would shout out, chuck things back and forth, answer back, engage in loud private conversations and, in general, make the teacher's job almost impossible.

The teacher would try to present a subject, but how could a kid be expected to follow along? Due to the constant disruptions I found it hard to follow the lesson plans myself! Imagine if you went to a movie and that every five minutes the film would break and you then had to wait two or three minutes for the projectionist to get the film going again. Could you, no matter how exciting or dramatic the story was, get into that movie? I'm sure that you'll admit that it would be very, very difficult! The same thing happened to the students in these classrooms. I felt sorry for both the students who came to school wanting to learn as well as for the teachers who were trying so desperately to teach. With all these constant interruptions and the total lack of continuity the educational process took a backseat to a million little dramas and petty squabbles.

Kids were being sent to the office, sent out into the hallway, and sent in mid-class to other teacher's classrooms; discipline was an ever-present, all encompassing problem.

Every day many students were suspended. It started the first thing every morning, right after the pledge of allegiance, as large numbers had shown up out of dress code. It continued throughout the day as students talked back or even threatened teachers and indulged in all the shenanigans mentioned above. The culprits would return to the classes already in progress from the office waving their suspension forms on high, like a badge of honor, as the suspensions never went into effect until the following school day.

I noticed that the children behaved differently depending on what type of teacher was in the room. Young, pretty teachers seemed to have more success with the kids whereas fat, old, frumpy teachers had many more problems with class management.

These older gray haired ladies tended to be the ones with the wildest classes. Also, substitute teachers couldn't keep the classes under control at all. When the subs were supposed to be in control, with very few exceptions, the kids would act like a barrel of monkeys screaming and hollering and running around. Although the sub would yell and yell at them the class would never behave. As a para, I hated being in classrooms where that was happening. Many times the teachers would leave the classroom, for bathroom breaks or errands, leaving me in control and I would have major problems! Maybe because I was an older individual it didn't seem like the kids had much respect for me. In many ways, I'm sorry to say, they kind of treated me the same way that they mistreated the substitutes! In speaking with the kids I soon learned that many of them didn't have grandparents in their lives and most of their parents were only in their 20's and 30's so older people had a certain strangeness to them. When I was supposed to be in "control" I would watch things slide, inexorably, into chaos and I'd find myself staring at the clock and praying for the teacher's return as my shouts bounced harmlessly off the kid's ears.

Many of my fellow paras, all of whom were much younger than me and all of whom were either black or Hispanic, seemed to have some misgivings as to whether I was going to last in the job or not. They advised me that I was too soft spoken and stated that I would have to learn to holler louder. That one thing I would definitely recommend if you want to get a job as a para in an inner-city school; you'd better have a voice like a Marine Corp. drill sergeant! Otherwise the kids won't listen. As a matter of fact some of the assistant principals would even walk up and down the hallways screaming into megaphones. Megaphones apparently are a big, big help in getting the kids from one place to another and many times are the only way to be heard over the din.

The constant screaming at the kids is all you hear all day long, six hours a day.

The teachers and principals scream at the kids. The kids scream and yell at each other and the staff; so, in general, unless you have a pair of earplugs; it's a terrible place to be! Teachers complained that the parents of students who were constantly disruptive and frequently suspended seldom attended open house nights. Notes sent home were usually ignored and parent 'phone numbers for contact purposes were often disconnected or obsolete. One mother who was finally contacted after days of dodging calls about her assaultive daughter shouted to the teacher: "Why you call me on this number?" (Which was her cell phone number). "You wastin' my minutes. Don't ever call me on this number again. I don't wanna hear about this baloney." This was a parent's response regarding a serious issue involving her child; actually two children because her daughter had gotten into a fight. I was beginning to realize that maybe the reason that my school (and maybe twenty others in my city) was failing might be traced back to failing parents!

Do you know which parents would come to the scheduled parent teacher meetings every couple of months? It would be the parents of the few good students who would be unfortunate enough to be in this hellhole of a school. Talk about preaching to the choir!

These were the students I felt profoundly sorry for. It was hard for me to adapt to my new situation. All my life I've loved learning. I've read thousands of books and I constantly peruse the Internet to try and learn even more; but these kids actively hated learning. Many of them hated it with a passion and were resistant to it. Teachers would try their best to cram knowledge into their closed, know-it-all little minds; but being as learning adverse as they were; these kids would pick up on any excuse to disrupt the class, start trouble and cause a commotion..

One boy named Joe who would constantly dress like an NBA basketball star with all the bling and jewelry around his neck, kind of a big gorilla of a character, was a good example of what I've been talking about. When the science teacher, Ms. Rostof we'll call her, tried to teach the class about the moon's effect on tides, Joe sitting in the back row began to scream: "What do we gotta know about tides for? Do we have 'em around here?" Now keep in mind that our city is about fifty miles from the nearest ocean and as Ms. Rostof patiently tried to explain this fact to the wondering class, Joe bellowed out again, "If we don't have 'em around here, what the hell we gotta learn about them for!'

This was a boy who wrote down on his science quiz that the moon was the other side of the sun! "Da side u c at nite", as he wrote it. Dear readers this was happening in an eighth grade science class ! Most of them were shocked when Ms. Rostof and I explained to them that the earth revolved around the sun, the vast majority believed, as of course their ancestors did in medieval times, that the sun revolved around the earth. With infinite patience, Ms. Rostof would show them solar system models but the little scholars would usually take them apart when she had her head turned, and throw the little planets and moons around as if they were billiard balls!

I felt sorry for Ms. Rostof. She was one of my favorite teachers. She worked so hard to keep the kids interested and work with them despite their active aversion to learning. She would constantly show them videos that she had downloaded from You-tube or "Mythbusters" demonstrating to them interesting scientific experiments and make every attempt to get them hooked on science while, unfortunately, the majority of the class could care less. As she showed the videos, I could see as a para stationed in the back of the classroom, notes were being passed back and forth, kids were whispering, kids were flirting; people were doing mostly anything possible except paying attention. It was my job to put a stop to these activities, but if I shouted at every kid doing them the class would be disrupted even more, so I soon learned, for the sake of the few students that were in there trying to learn, to ignore about 90% of what I saw.

I'll never forget the day when she showed the children pictures of her beautiful beachfront home in Rhode Island using Google Earth and our bling covered gorilla in the back row yelled out: "Da ain't yo house! Give me a break. You jus a teacher an' a teacher don't make dat kinda money. You can't afford a house like dat! It probly belongs to some basketball player or sumptin. What did you pay for it, twenty-five cent?" Ms. Rostof had tears in her eyes, all her years of hard work were being totally denigrated by this moron gorilla. She asked me to remove him from the class and I did.

I brought him to the library and said " Joe, how could you say something like that to your teacher?" "Ah, she full of shit", he said. I said, "Well Joe that's not true, I'm sure that is her beach house." "I don't wanna hear it, she don't play basketball, she not in Hollywood, she can't have a house like dat". Unfortunately this was his, as well as many of his fellow students', belief.

Now we must keep in mind that these children are America's future. Regrettably their ignorance is abysmal. I'll never forget another time in Ms. Rostof's class right before Thanksgiving break, a black girl was talking to a white girl. The black one said to the white, "Whatjew gonna be doin' Friday"? "Friday after Thanksgiving?" the white one replied, "I'll be goin' shoppin!" "You can't do that," her black friend answered in all hurt seriousness, "Dat's black Friday, only Black people can go shoppin' on dat day." Another time while working with Jose in Math class, we were trying to go over the multiplication tables which very few of these children knew. Now again, we're talking sixth, seventh and eighth grade here. Many of them were as old as fourteen and fifteen. Most of them had the latest cellphones and I-pods, although they were strictly forbidden to use these devices in school, actually courting suspension for having these gadgets with them, and the latest sneakers to boot, but parents apparently never brought them flash cards to learn their number facts. This is something which, as far as I could see, never ever happened because not one in twenty knew them. Anyways, as I say, while working with Jose one day I asked him what four times four was. "Fifteen", he confidently shouted; I said "Jose, the answer is sixteen". "Mr. Shine, I was close, I was close, I should get credit! I was close!" I patiently tried to explain to him that close is only good in horseshoes, not math, but my logic seemed to fall on deaf ears. Despite their lack of academic knowledge and their profound hatred of it the kids did, however; know all about the new movies that were coming out each weekend, all the latest gossip on Hollywood celebrities, who was winning or losing on "American Idol" and all the Pop Culture kind of things that America is so obsessed with. They dressed in the latest clothes and styles but when it came to history, math or reading, forget it!

Jose was a skinny little thing and you could tell that God had not been kind in his physical makeup. Yet he would constantly scream: "Hold me back Mr. Shine I'm gonna attack him, I'm gonna attack him!" while running at some big kid twice his size. It was kind of funny in a way, but also sad. Later he began bringing sweets and baked goods from home to try and curry favor with all the big, more with it kids who often picked on him. After the Haitian earthquake Jose, who was very proud of his Puerto Rican heritage, told us that immediately after the earthquake that all the able-bodied men in Puerto Rico had jumped into the ocean and swam to Haiti to help out. Not many in the class believed him but some did. He would constantly say, "I'm from the 'hood, I'm from the 'hood, dats why I'm tough". He thought it was a badge of honor to be proud of that he was from "da hood". Unfortunately some of his fellow students disagreed with him they'd say, "You not from da hood". But he'd shoot back: "Yah, I'm from da hood, I was born in da hood, and I live in da hood so I'm from da hood"! Apparently, in these kid's minds, being from "da hood" is a good thing.

Sometimes students would ask me if I was from the "hood." I would tell them that I wasn't from the "hood" and they would immediately begin to look at me in a different light. Students who received good marks were picked on; nobody was more hated than the nerd. A child who was conscientious, brought his notebook to class every day and tried to pay attention in class was generally pelted with spitballs, pushed around in the hallways and treated as if he had wandered into the wrong school!

Although my school was a sad and loud place I never had a day where I didn't find some humor in the ridiculous comments that the students, in all seriousness, would make.

I remember Brandy, a sixteen year old girl in seventh grade, who definitely was a lower functioning student. I recall being informed by the special education supervisor that her I.Q. was on the low side of eighty. I'll never forget the time when I was trying to use logic to teach Brandy what classes of objects were; for example types of flowers, dandelions, roses, violets and so on. I asked her if she knew about wars like World War II and the Civil War, hoping that she might mention Iraq or Afghanistan or maybe the troubles we were having with Iran. At least some war happening in the Middle East so I was shocked when she said "Hawaii."

I said, "Hawaii, Brandy I don't think that there's been wars over in Hawaii recently."

"Oh, Mr. Shine where you been? All the girls over there been fightin' over the bachelor! It's the biggest war I ever seen."

Another time sitting next to Jose, another source of humor for me, although it was of course totally unintentional, I noticed him starring out the window during class as if in a deep daydream. "Jose", I said to him. "Pay attention, the teacher is trying to teach something here." But he just ignored me, as the teacher droned on and on while being entirely ignored by almost the entire class. "Mr. Shine, Mr. Shine," he shouted, "The cloud, the cloud!" (As he pointed to a cloud out the window) What's the matter Jose?" I patiently asked puzzled by his preoccupation with a simple cloud. "Mr. Shine the cloud's MOVING MOVING", he stuttered in amazement. "Jose, clouds always move." "Oh." It really wouldn't have been funny if Jose hadn't have been in the sixth grade!

3

Good Teachers

Many of the teachers there, as I mentioned before were really quite good. Again changing the names to protect the innocent (and the guilty) I might want to give credit to Ms. Brenner, Ms. Rasaad, and Ms. Rodriquez who were all very competent teachers. They knew how to control their classes well and when they were teaching there was only a minimum amount of disruption going on to my everlasting pleasure and surprise. These teachers were tough, yet affectionate, and they always helped to build up their student's self esteem. At first I thought this might have been a problem, that they're always emphasizing self-esteem. Back in my day, again I went to parochial schools, the nuns weren't at all shy about telling us how stupid we were, or taking us to the back of the classroom and giving us a good whipping if we needed it. I personally thought that this had helped me immensely in my educational background; of course this type of thing never happened any more as physical punishment is now totally forbidden in modern schools, and the emphasis is on self-esteem and self-confidence. So no matter how dumb these students were, the teachers would always praise them to the skies and build up their self-confidence.

This is good in a way though, although at first I thought it might be a problem, but I soon began to realize that actually it was a good thing. These students were able in many many ways to overcome their negative home background issues because of the self-confidence that these (and earlier) teachers had instilled in them. Kids who were dumb as bricks had tremendous amounts of self-confidence and walked around feeling as if they could do anything! These teachers brought out the best in their students by constantly praising them and making them feel as if they could accomplish a lot and even the worst ones would pay attention most of the time and the class would be under some modicum of control. The kids may have not been interested in what the teacher was saying but at least there was enough quiet in the classroom that those few students who were actually there for an education could at least listen. The young teachers, many of them black or Hispanic, had the same background as their charges themselves often having grown up in the "hood." The students identified well with these teachers and the teachers identified well with them. The teachers who had grown up like the students in the ghetto could reach and inspire the kids in ways that neither I nor any of the other middle class background staff could. They were able to use peer pressure to keep the class under control. Sometimes when kids would misbehave they'd be able to use humor to defuse situations. Other times they'd get the kids themselves to turn on the troublemakers and make those acting out kids feel foolish. So loud mouthed kids found it advantageous to be quiet in their classrooms. These types of teachers were the best teachers at the inner city school.

I remember, for example, one time Ms. Brenner was confronting one of the numerous students in her class who had verbal diarrhea and she said to him: "I talked to yo Mama."

As she often did she kind of rolled her voice down into a ghetto type slang as she talked to him not reflective of her speech to me or any other fellow teachers. "I talked to yo Mama an' she told me I could put duct tape on yo mouth if you keep interruptin'the class." "Oh, no Ms. Brennner, I won't interrup anymore!" he stammered back fearfully. Now I'm sure that it was all a ruse and that she had never gotten permission from the mother to put duct tape on the boy's mouth and of course she certainly never would do so even if she had, as it would never be allowed at our school. But she had the boy half believing that she was going to put duct tape on his mouth. "No, please, don't put duck tape on my mouth!" After that whenever he started going off again in class she'd say, "remember the duck tape." Even other kids would taunt him saying, "Be quiet remember duct tape" and so she managed to get that kid, who was totally mouthy in every other class, to at least be quiet in her class. She often used ruses to keep the kids in line. Boys who were "tough guys" she'd challenge to meet her for an out and out fight out by the flagpole at the end of school. Again, a totally implausible scenario, but the little nitwits often believed her and started behaving better. Misbehaving students were often told to go and stand in the hallway. Sometimes I was told to get them out of their seats and to walk them out into the hallway or to the principal's office. One frequent problem that we ran into was that we were not allowed to touch the students and so sometimes they'd just refuse to leave their seats, causing all the other kids to laugh and making the disruption last longer. There was a police officer assigned to our school but he never seemed to around when we needed him.

Ms. Brenner, as she often did, had an ingenious solution to this problem. When she would ask a defiant little sixth grader to get out of his seat and stand in the hallway and he would respond to her; "You can't make me move, you can't touch me" she'd answer "Well I can't, but I can get somebody who can"! Then she'd walk down the hall to an eighth grade classroom and come back with two enormous six foot hoodlums (who were probably 16 years old) and she'd tell them; "Pick that student's desk up, with him sitting in it, and put it in the hallway." "No, no", the little miscreant would scream, "I'll go stand in the hall. I'll go stand in the hall." And so the problem would be solved.

The response of the student, who didn't want to move though, is reflective of one of the biggest problems that we had. The children were hyper sensitive about their rights and all day long I and my fellow paras heard from the kids; "You can't touch me" or" You can't make me", and this made discipline almost impossible to enforce so I sometimes wondered why we were there at all! The teachers had a little more leverage in that they had the power of the grade book and the ability to call the parents, but that leverage too slipped with many students. As I mentioned before, many of the parents of these kids could care less about how their sons and daughters did in school, and would refuse to answer 'phone calls or come to meetings. This family attitude that education was unimportant was alive and well in these monster students who were unfazed by the fact that they were flunking classes, so the grade book leverage too was unavailing. Of course these bad apples knew well that despite their teacher's threats that they would probably be advanced to the next grade come June, as the whole school operated on the "social promotion" principal. Every year I was there only 20 or 25 students out of the 500 students that I worked with were actually held back despite the fact that hundreds of them got only 30's or 40's for legitimate grades throughout the year. When I asked the teachers why this was happening they admitted that they were pressured to pass the kids by the administration. "Besides," they would tell me, "Do you want to see these monsters here again next year?" The attitude seemed to be, hey the city can't afford to build any more new schools, so we have to kick these bozos upstairs to make room for the next platoon of idiots that's coming in! The teachers had many tricks to fool themselves into believing that these kids, despite their horrific grades, deserved to pass. They would grade on a curve, let 60 be the lowest score posted (even if the student got a 10), drop grades that were bad and allow re-tests and do-overs. Almost all the tests were open-book, students were allowed to take tests home or to the library to work on, and more importantly, teachers looked the other way when I or other paras fed students the correct answers! Academically these spawn of the ghetto may have been completely lost, but they definitely had "street smarts" and they knew how the system worked. They knew darned well that the odds were pretty good that they were going to get promoted despite their bad grades and their teachers threats, so they just let the threats bounce off their backs like water off a duck! What did they think of out of school suspensions? No big deal, those were opportunities to have little mini-vacations and to stay home and play video games. Many kids came back from their suspensions with rewards their parents bought them while they were out like new tattoos, watches or bling. One student they had me doing a one on one was missing 93 out of 180 days of school but he was still promoted to the seventh grade! So, dear reader as you can see, maintaining any kind of discipline or learning environment was almost an impossibility under the conditions that we were working under. If you were clever like Ms. Brenner or if the kids liked you well, maybe, maybe you could do something; otherwise forget it!

One other aspect of working with the kids that I'd like to go back to at this point is the fact that they were all so puffed up with self-confidence and self-esteem (although as I said in general those are good things) that they were extraordinarily difficult to correct even when they were wrong. One time Jose told me that he had spent the entire weekend working on his grandfather's 1864 Volkswagen. I patiently explained to him that there were no 1864 cars, that cars hadn't been invented yet then, that he must have meant his grand-dad's 1964 Volkswagen but he refused to accept my correction. No matter how I remonstrated with him I could never shake him from the belief that I was wrong and he was right, and that it was an 1864 Volkswagen! Of course Jose was a bit of a storyteller and it's quite possible that his grandfather didn't even have a

Volkswagen, but I'm sure you get the point. It wasn't just Jose, all the kids were like that; hide bound in their belief in totally untrue and ridiculous things.

Part of the problem might have gone back to their teachers. When the teachers would ask the kids to write something I would go around the room and try to help them with their spelling which was unbelievably atrocious. The teachers didn't like that at all and would stop me! The teachers claimed it wasn't important at all how the kids spelled or miss-spelled words the important thing is what they "were trying to say." Maybe they thought that students would be too discouraged if there was an emphasis on their spelling and they wouldn't write as much (not that these kids ever wrote more than a few sentences anyways) but for whatever reason most of the teachers wouldn't let me help them out. One teacher, Ms. Brooks, actually hollered at me: "Mr. Shine don't tell them how to spell the words, there are dictionaries in the back of the room they can use if they want." Of course that didn't work out too well, the kids were too lazy to go looking through dictionaries, they just shrugged and went back to scribbling fragments down that may, or may not, have meant something! In defense of the kids, sometimes the kids would ask me how to spell the word in a real low voice so the teacher couldn't hear that they were asking and I could help them that way. How the teacher could understand, much less grade, these chopped up botched up "essays" was a perpetual wonderment to me. I forgot to point out that the kids' punctuation and grammar was as bad as their spelling. The teachers did try to work on these points a little but again, the emphasis always seemed to be on what the student was trying to say as opposed to what he actually did write. Teachers leapt for joy if a kid wrote a paragraph even if it was full of first-grader type miss-spellings, no capitalization and no punctuation. Speaking of dictionaries we spent months working with the students in a remedial reading class called "Reading 180" where we tried to teach the students to use dictionaries with limited success. The problem with a dictionary is that you have to know how to spell the word (at least a little bit) in order to use it. Even looking up the meaning of words given to them on handouts was very difficult for them and they constantly needed my help. "Sing the alphabet in your head, Sing the alphabet in your head", I'd shout at my chowderhead charges hour after hour, morning after morning. As I say, looking up words in the dictionary turned out to be a monumental task for many of them.

James W. Shine

Another thing I noticed about the modern educational system was the copious use of handouts. My school alone, with no exaggeration, went through twenty tons of copier paper and two hundred pounds of ink a year! Every teacher during all seven periods, the very first thing they did when the kids walked in the door of the classroom, was to give each one a handout. One of my jobs was to help pass these out and then to collect them at the end of the period. I, and the other paras, spent hours at the Xerox machine making the literally thousands and thousands of copies that the teachers needed on a weekly basis. How did the kids treat these handouts? Not too well, a good 20 or 30 percent of them ended up on the floor after each period and, I swear, out of 30 students in each class at least 4 or 5 of them came back with no names on them when I collected them. Another one of my daily shouts was: "Don't forget to put your names on them!" Most of the students, I noticed, would just glance at them and then in a haphazard manner fill in whatever answers they might know or just stick into the blanks key phrases or words regurgitated from their textbooks. The vast majority of the kids weren't even careful about copying down the answers (usually highlighted in red or bold black) from the books correctly. Words and phrases that should have been copied from the texts verbatim onto the handouts were, as likely as not, miss-spelled and had parts missing. Slapdash, sloppy work seemed to be the hallmark of the day. The following day if I questioned the kids about what was on the handouts the day before, few of them seemed to have any clue.

How different this all was from my junior high school (equivalent to middle school) back in my youth! The nuns would say the words or phrases and then write them on the blackboard for us as they were speaking, and then have us copy them down. It was very rare for us to get a mimeograph, instead we would write everything, copying it off the blackboard. That way the information would go into our little minds by way of three channels; we'd hear the nuns speak it, we'd have to look at it closely on the board so we could copy it down, and finally the muscles of our hands would write the letters and transfer the information to out brains. The kids in my school hardly ever were asked to copy anything at all; everything was stuck in front of them with these stupid handouts. I began to wonder if maybe the reason why my kids couldn't read or write as well as their peers in the suburbs was the fact that they had never spent any time copying correct phrases and sentences! In the spring when the CAP and CMT tests were done my suspicions were given credence. Despite the fact that the administration pulled one hundred of the worst students out of the tests to jack up the scores, my school fell a full twenty percentage points below the statewide averages in proficiency in reading and math. Among my eight grade science students only 47% of those tested (and again many were not tested or were given easier tests for special ed kids) were proficient. No wonder I was sitting in the middle of a failing school! I would joke with the teacher that now we have"smartboards" that it was too bad that we didn't have smart students to go with them. But when I suggested to the young teachers that maybe it would be better if we would make the students copy down the information instead of using all these handouts they would just look at me as if I were some sort of old fogy that had wandered in from a by-gone century.

One day after a particularly difficult class when the kids had really tested her skills to their absolute maximum, I said to Ms.. Brenner: "Have you ever considered making it easier for yourself and going out to teach in the suburbs"? She answered, "No Mr. Shine, this is right where I belong and this is right where I want to stay. I enjoy working with these kids." My hat is off to her and to the many other teachers like her. People who may say that this book is negative are 100% wrong; I salute the teachers that are working hard in the inner-city schools. They have been blamed and stigmatized unfairly for the failures of the system and their students' lack of achievement. In most cases it is not their fault. They have fought a long difficult up-hill battle against the myriad of problems I've been referring to and been given little thanks or appreciation by the public.

4

The Not So Good Teachers

In contrast to Ms. Brenner, let's take a look on the other hand, at a different teacher that was not doing as well, we'll call her "Mrs. McGinty." Like myself she was an older person and teaching was a second career for her. Like myself, technology had left her behind, originally she had been a travel agent, but just as the Internet had put me out of business at my discount brokerage job, so the Internet had put her out of business at her full-service travel agency. Deciding in her fifties to go into teaching she ended up, as I did, at this inner-city school where there was almost a total disconnect between her and her students. Her classroom was complete chaos. Kids were screaming, hollering, yelling, jumping up and down and running in and out of the classroom door while acting like she wasn't present in the room at all! Part of the problem was that she couldn't remember their names. Again that's not surprising; you have to realize that these teachers had to memorize 150 names on a daily basis. The kids rotated through in classes of 30 per class throughout five periods per day and with the strangest sort of names that they have now-a-days it would try anyone's ability to remember them all. But when she would shout at a student, the student would say to her: "That's not my name, you got me wrong, " Let's not forget that these kids with their emphasis on self confidence would, even if you did remember their name, if you mispronounced it in the slightest way, instead of addressing the issue that you brought up with them about their misbehavior, would correct you or the teacher about the fact that their name had been mispronounced. Eventually I was very happy when the administration had mercy on me, and reassigned me to another classroom and I no longer had to work with her. Being in her class was a horrific nightmare; she may as well have thrown her lesson plans into the trash every day when she walked in, because for her the kids acted like a barrel of monkeys, and no learning happened in there whatsoever.

Another bad teacher, we'll call her "Mrs. Retchard", was also an older white woman who in this case had been teaching for about twenty years; but unlike Mrs.McGinty she had good classroom management skills. The kids did behave for her, sometimes it seemed as if they were a little afraid, but her class was as boring as wheat toast! All during the twenty years she had been teaching she had been using the exact same syllabus and there was very little in there connecting with kids today in modern times or relating her history lessons to current events. The students found her lectures to be not in the least bit interesting and generally slept quietly through them, which didn't seem to faze her in the least! Mrs. Retchard definitely didn't want any input from me as a paraprofessional. At one point after one of her classes, I diplomatically asked her if she would be willing to make some changes in the well-worn syllabus that she'd been using; in her discussion about the Civil War she had told the kids that Texas had not been part of the Confederacy! After a quick visit to the school library, I had brought her a map showing that, indeed, Texas had been a part of the Confederacy, and that she had unfortunately been wrong in what she had been teaching. She became enraged at me, sputtered and sputtered, turned on her heel, and stomped away! The next day the assistant principal, who was my ultimate supervisor, called me into his office and told me that Mrs. Retchard was unhappy with my services, and that I was being re-assigned to another teacher. Apparently at Williams Middle School, paraprofessionals were not expected to know anything, especially not enough where they'd be able to correct a teacher. My fellow paras were shocked at my behavior in Mrs. Retchard's class; none of them had ever dared to speak up in a classroom, and many of them warned me that I was jeopardizing my job by acting the way I did. Throughout my years of service there I ignored my well meaning co-workers advice, and continued to speak up in whatever classroom I found myself in; as I reasoned that in most cases the teachers I was working for were my children's age, and I had a lifetime worth of experience behind me so darn it, somebody was going to listen!

Fortunately some teachers did utilize this old gray head's knowledge. I'll never forget that when Barack Obama was elected Ms. Rodriquez asked me if I would give a speech about him as she admitted that she didn't know that much about his background. I happily did so, explaining to the kids that he had come from a family with an unwed mother, that he had been teased as a young man about his unusual name, and that he loved basketball and still played it every day so as to keep in shape. To avoid ridicule he had told his fellow middle school students to call him "Barry" as his real Muslim name hadn't gone over so well in Hawaii, and he loved technology and all the latest gadgets. The kids gave me a standing ovation and cheered and stamped their feet so loud that the principal came running in from the hallway to see what was the matter! The kids loved Barack Obama passionately. The inner city black and Hispanic kids could really identify with him and he was a great role model for them. Whatever he may or may not do as President, just the fact that he got elected restored the American dream and proved that it was for everyone. As I told the kids in my speech, his election proved that anyone could do it; make it straight to the top, whether you were black, Hispanic, from a broken home or the ghetto, there were no excuses anymore, as racism was in the past; for their generation there were only green lights and unlimited potential if they were willing to work hard. I told them that Barack Obama had worked hard, that he had always been at the top of his class, and that he and his economically struggling mother had worked every night until midnight on his homework, and when that was not enough they got up and continued at 4 am, and that's why he was where he was. Like I said they gave me a standing ovation so I know that these kids can be inspired.

But in general, the young teachers at the school seemed to take the attitude that a sixty year old, fat white haired old man such as myself, should basically just sit in the back of the room and not say very much. As I had been a fighter all my life I did, however, rebel against this treatment.

Sometimes my job was rewarding, I would walk around the class and peer over the children's shoulders while trying to help them with math. I would coach them and try to help them remember the math facts that they usually forgot, showed them how to do long division, and helped them with their schoolwork on a one on one basis. Unfortunately some teachers even took exception to me doing that! Ms. Brooks had a wonderful relationship with the kids. She was a beautiful woman in her mid-thirties, had been an unwed mother as a teenager but yet had managed to turn her life around, had put herself through school and now, in the kids' eyes at least, had become a big success. The students really admired her although she was tough as nails and never put up with any nonsense. Her 18-year-old son was already starting college, yet she was still an attractive young woman in the prime of life. Having come from an inner-city background she really "clicked" with the kids and her classroom was under complete control. Of all the teachers I worked with (and I worked with dozens) she seemed to be among the best when it came to classroom management skills. Yet she seemed to take umbrage when I'd try to help the kids with their abominable spelling or their hopeless or non-existent punctuation. She's the one, as I mentioned before, who would shout that they should use a dictionary. She seemed to ignore the fact that they hardly ever did so! Maybe she felt, as her classroom was always under great control, that it was unnecessary (and maybe even a little bit divisive) to have another adult in the room.

To her credit though I'll never forget the time when I did take it upon myself to speak up in her class. Because I had invested well and had a certain amount of savings; something that these cash-strapped young teachers who looked down on me did not (they were always complained that they were struggling under massive student loans); I had a fearlessness that my fellow paras were unable to share. I suppose it came from the job security that a nice bank account gives you, although my wife was mad when I told her about this episode. So as I say, I really didn't care if I stepped on some toes or even if I got fired from this job! Although I knew she didn't want me speaking up, at one point when she was lecturing about racial discrimination down in the south back in "the old days", as a matter of fact she had shown the kids a movie about this subject; I boldly interrupted the discussion. I told the children about the time when I was twelve years old- about their age's now- and I had taken a car trip through the old south with my parents. The interstate highway system had not yet been completed and I had seen with my own eyes the white and colored only restrooms and lunch counters that the film had been talking about, and I had seen the tar paper shacks that the blacks had been forced to live in, so they should know that these things were not just boring, ancient history, but actual events that had been witnessed by somebody still among us. I explained to them that it was because of those horrible conditions and that repressive discrimination that their grandparents had left the south to escape to our Northern city for the job opportunities we had back then. The kids listened closely and many of them were extremely interested, but as often happened when I, the old man, began to speak some of the young wiseacres began making fun of me so Ms. Brooks shouted out "Quiet, an adult is speaking." I definitely had to give her credit that day for letting me have some input when she thought it was appropriate to do so.

I got the impression that almost all of these kids had been horribly spoiled by their parents. Although their parents gave them, despite their ostensible poverty, the latest style clothing and electronic gadgets; I could tell by their total lack of impulse control that they had not been raised as I, or my siblings, had raised our children. One of the saddest things I noticed was that the teachers could no longer have discussions with them. Back when I was going to school we had conversations with our teachers. That's because, back in those days, one child would speak at a time! We used to raise our hands and wait to be recognized by the teacher before we could speak. That way we would learn from other kids' experiences as well as from the teacher's. The staff at Williams tried to get the kids to raise their hands too, but it always seemed to go off the rails! All the kids would try to speak at once, and it often ended up with such a total babble that no one could understand what anyone else was saying. The idea of letting one person speak, and other people be silent, is something that these kids have a very, very, hard time doing. Children shouted over one another when anyone tried to speak, or made fun of each other the minute a fellow classmate opened their mouths; so class "discussions" generally degenerated into loud arguments and shouting matches ending with very little knowledge imparted and bad feelings the predominant memory. Of course some of the teachers at the school were neither good nor bad they were, as the Italians would say, "mes a mes."

5

Noise and Chaos

At lunchtime I would have café duty. Five hundred kids at a time would come in, Indian file by classroom, into the enormous café and sit at the long tables. The principal and assistant principals would be screaming at them through bullhorns: "Keep it down, keep it down, the noise is too much." As the bedlam wouldn't even be dialed down a notch, they'd start threatening to impose a "silent" café. We would have to have a "silent" café. But every day the noise continued to be too loud so half the time the so-called "silent" cafes had to be implemented, for all the actual good they did. Unfortunately, I noticed when I was late in arriving, I could never tell just by listening whether or not a "silent" café was happening! These students could never get it through their thick heads that there was a difference between screaming and talking. The only setting on their volume control was "loud." I used to tell them "You should study whispering 101." The idea of whispering was totally foreign to them unless a drug deal or beat down was being planned! They would always shout in loud voices causing the maximum amount of disruption and making it almost impossible for the teachers to teach.

    Teachers and the school administration were obsessed with the Connecticut Mastery Test (CMT). Every spring our failing school, together with all the other schools in Connecticut, had to take this test. So the teachers spent a lot of time coaching the kids for this all-important exam. Desperate to come out well on the CMT one of the schools in my city was found to be actually cheating to pass! As the State was curious as to how a failing school could post such good results they went back and looked at the test papers and found erasure marks changing wrong answers into right ones. They also found two sets of handwriting in the booklets where apparently teachers filled in responses to questions that the students had ignored or where they elaborated on fragmented pieces of answers that the kids had scribbled down. Seventeen teachers and administrators were suspended without pay at that school only a couple of miles away from Williams, and I wouldn't be surprised if out and out cheating to make the students look better was happening throughout my district. As billions of dollars of federal education funds are based on these tests, and teachers and administrators feel their jobs are on the line, cheating has become a nationwide problem since the "No Child Left Behind" law has been implemented. In Atlanta scores of teachers have been suspended and the whole city school system is being investigated. At Williams I didn't personally witness the staff going to these extremes but the teachers did spend months "teaching to the test" as they called it, taking away from what precious little educational time they had. The goal was to have us make "Adequate Yearly Progress" (AYP) as otherwise we would fall even further down in the failing schools category that we were already mired in. Even that was difficult. They would spend all their time going over sample CMT questions, possible CMT questions, good test-taking techniques and so on frantically trying to boost test scores. During the ten days in April when the CMTs were being held, they tried to put Williams under the strictest control. I often thought it was a joke that they had to have such rigid discipline during the CMTs, while the rest of the year discipline was so lax. As anyone who has had anything to do with kids will tell you, you can't have that type of herky-jerky approach and be successful. You have to be consistent! While the tests were in progress they'd use the carrot and the stick. Kids would be given sugary treats and goodies to eat; they'd have dances and pep rallies and whatever else they could think of to psych them up and get them in the mood to take the CMTs. Contrariwise, bad behaviors that would be ignored during the rest of the year drew fast suspensions during these all important tests! Because we were in a failing school the administration knew well how much was riding on these results. The whole reputation of our school was on the line! Unfortunately every year I was there we continued to fail. As we were in a failing school, the parents of my students under the "No Child Left Behind" act had the right to get special tutoring for their kids, or even to remove them from Williams altogether and place them in a better school where maybe they could get a better education. In short these parents had many, many options. But again we have to remember that we are dealing here with parents who seldom, if ever, attend teacher-parent counseling meetings, parents who don't answer telephone calls, and who are generally so removed from their kids educational process that all the "rights" given to them in this well-meaning law will actually do their children no good whatsoever. So the parents of the kids in the left- behind schools are going to keep those kids left behind! The principal of our school, we'll call him "Doctor Padula", seemed like a nice fellow.

He obviously was totally immersed in the CMTs. I'll never forget the time a boy was brought to his office by an assistant principal because the boy had attacked another student and Doctor Padula's first remark to his assistant was: "Has this boy finished his CMTs?" The school obviously had to keep its priorities straight!

The administration had ways of gaming the testing system. A lot of the special education students that I worked with took an easier version of the

CMT called the Modified Assessment System (MAS) test. Also in many cases, the lower functioning students test scores were ignored altogether or were taken out of the calculations pertaining to the school.

At the school end-of-the year celebration party Doctor Padula got up to give a speech describing how well he thought things had gone throughout the year that we had just finished. As he pontificated about his and our professionalism, dedication and so on, he bloviated that we always should remember that: "Ninety-Nine and a half percent of all the kids we deal with are good kids. Never forget that!" I remember that I, and the rest of the paras, looked at one another and started laughing. We shook our heads asking ourselves, "What school is that man working at"? Doctor Padula was making $140,000 per year, seven times what we were, but he either had no clue as to what was going on in his school, or else he had to blindly spout some party line given to him from high above. Either way he was totally disconnected from reality. And the sad part was, he was our leader!

The following year, possibly due to his good work (?), Doctor Padula was promoted to be one of our city's three high school principals. He was replaced by Mr. Ripello, who at least was a little bit more realistic. For example, at the opening of the school year seminar the year he started, he gave us some good practical advice. He told us that if we ever completely lost our temper and said "Hakeem, you're an asshole!" and then Hakeem (or whatever student we were screaming at) said: "What did you say?" we should come back quickly with "Hakeem, I said you're a hassle!" He even admitted that he was glad to "see the backsides" of the eighth grade class from hell that was there on my very first year. A man who didn't spend all his time looking through rose-colored glasses (unlike his predecessor) he later began to implement some major changes that greatly improved our school. But more about that in a following chapter!

6
M&M

I helped the teachers correct the kids' papers and I saw that in each class a large percentage of them (somewhere between 30-40%) would get 30's and 40's and 50's on their test scores throughout the year so I was shocked at the end of the year, that of the 150 kids I worked with in Yeshiva's house, only ten or fifteen were being retained. All the rest were being passed! As I mentioned before social promotion was happening at Williams Middle School in a big way and that the administration was forcing the teachers to pass them through.

They knew that because neither they, nor I, wanted to see these bozos all day long for another year, and our struggling city couldn't afford to build enough schools to hold them all, we had to kick them upstairs to make room for the next platoon of idiots!

I never forget that I especially questioned Ms. Rostoff about a kid I'll "M&M." M&M was a white boy but I've never seen a white boy adapt to ghetto life as completely as he did! Tattooed from head to toe and sporting earrings, gold chains and all other sorts of bling, he reminded me a lot of the real M&M out of Detroit. His entire language was a ghetto- speak and he was constantly resistant and obnoxious. Whenever I asked him to do anything his constant response was, "Why"? And if I told him why he had to do it, then he would come right out and flat out say, "I'm not doin' it!" He was constantly in trouble, being sent to the office for fighting, disrespecting paras or teachers, and generally was a total disaster for the school. His parents seemed to encourage him in his crazy ways, one time while being suspended from the school for fighting; he came back to school with three of four new tattoos as a reward. Most work, as I said before, he would simply refuse to do or if he did it at all, he would simply cheat by copying off other students. If we watched closely and prevented him from copying, he would do the very, very minimum when hard pressed, and usually get most of that wrong.

The worst things about him though, were his attitudes. I'll never forget around veteran's day, when we had some veterans come in and to talk about their sacrifices, there was even one who had lost an arm in Iraq; M&M said, "I don't want to see no damn veterans. What do I give a shit about them? What did they do for me? I don't give two shits about the US Army!" Mrs. Rosneff was so enraged she refused to let him attend the assembly (where he probably would have shouted insults to our wounded veterans up on the stage) and instead instructed me to take him to the library as I had often been forced to do in the past. At the library I asked him, "How can you say that about our soldiers?"

"Who gives a crap", he responded, "What did they do for me? What do they do for the 'hood?" That's what my friend M&M, who often called me "Uncle Chaalie," had to say about veteran's day. As a favor, Dear reader, I shall spare you this wonderful child's attitudes about religion and the traditional values that we all retain in our hearts. Following the rules was for "fools" he believed, because if you were "slick" as he put it, doing so was completely unnecessary.

At the end of the year I asked Mrs. Rosneff why he was being promoted. Not only that, he was even being permitted (despite having 36 suspensions for bad behavior throughout the year) to wear a cap and gown and to prance across the stage and grab his diploma!

She said that, despite the fact that his grades didn't justify it at all; the administration had mandated this. Considering his behavior and attitudes and his woeful grades I myself had mixed feelings about his going on. After all, he was almost sixteen years old, and at the rate his educational progress was going, he'd probably be about twenty-two if, and when, he ever did graduate from high school!

One of the most hilarious things is that my state recently passed a law making it mandatory now for children to attend school up until age seventeen. On the national level, President Obama wants to up the mandatory school age up to eighteen. What a hoot these ideas are! Previously these kids, who are deathly resistant to learning could drop out at sixteen, but now they can continue to be a drag on their fellow students who actually want to learn and on the whole educational establishment for massive more amounts of time. I suppose we can call it the "Teachers Full Employment Act."

Let's talk about the kids' attitudes a bit more. The ideas of the students were very very peculiar to me. First of all, they hated the police. Unlike myself, who when I went to school, we often had police come to the classroom, kind of an "Officer Friendly" type of thing; among the students I was working with hatred of police was quite common.

They said that the police had rousted them and that when they had gone downtown and visited our local mall; they were frequently thrown out by the mall security guards (whom they often mistook for police), so they didn't look upon the police as being any type of friends. They had very hostile attitudes towards not only the police, but towards anyone else in authority, whether that would be teachers, paras or any other adults in general.

The kids were extremely interested in the latest styles and fashions in sweaters, shoes, electronic gadgets and so on. Again, being typical Americans, the accoutrements were much more important to them than the substance. When I was young, we were told not to judge a book by its cover, but we very seldom hear that anymore in America now-a-days and our inner city middle school students certainly do judge books by their covers! Students were made fun of if they didn't wear the latest (and the most expensive) outfits. This mockery often applied to myself as well. I'd often hear, when I walked into the classroom, "You wearin' five dolla shoes there man." The wiseacres among the bunch looked at me with my out dated belt buckles, shoes and clothes as if this were a sign that I was some sort of a witless old fool. These things meant far more to them than any sort of knowledge that I might have had as an older person! Things are strictly judged in their world by appearances. But they were all up to date with the latest happenings among Hollywood's celebrities, the latest gossip, the latest news, and were just as smart as suburban kids were when it came to playing with the latest electronic gadgets.

7

Kevin and Friends

One of the students that I worked with quite frequently was named Kevin. Kevin was a nerd who was having an absolutely horrible time in middle school. In earlier years he had been physically bullied and pushed around, but now in eighth grade it was more psychological abuse that he was suffering from. I was often told to accompany him from class to class and I soon became basically his one friend. He reminded me a lot of myself when I was younger. Kevin was a smart kid and did well in school, especially distinguishing himself in science and math, but his problem was that he knew nothing about celebrities or sports, and had no interest in such things, so the kids treated him unmercifully. Whenever the teachers gave the children the opportunity to form groups and to work together on projects he was always excluded. He was basically shunned by all the other kids, and his middle school years were unhappy ones. Who says that children can't be cruel? If he had landed from Mars he would have probably fit in better than he did!

Hatred of older people was palpable. An example was Kara Cook, a young black girl with an IQ of about 80, who needed help in Math. Every time I'd go over to her desk to help her she'd say, "Get away from me! Go help somebody else, I don't need yo' help."

This was despite the fact that she was getting all of her Math problems wrong. The first time I tried to have a civil conversation with her, and to ignore her poor attitude, she shouted at me: "What are you doin' here? You so old you should be in a nursing home! Why ain't you in a nursing home? Tomorrow why don't you bring in your cane?"

Despite all this abuse I'd try my very best to work with her. I finally managed to get some type of rapprochement by pretending that I had known her grandfather who had died thirty years before she had been born. Then she began accepting my help, albeit on a somewhat hesitant and limited basis.

A typical class would go this way: the teacher would be talking in the front of the room, and I would be kind of wandering around toward the rear. I'd notice that a young girl was talking and not paying attention so I'd say to her, in a low voice, "Moesha, be quiet!" She'd quickly shout at me, "I'm not Moesha, I'm Monesha, why should I listen to you, you don't even know my name!" Then I'd say, "I'm sorry I got your name wrong Monesha, please be quiet." "I wasn't talkin'" Yes, you were, I heard you talking." "Everybody else is talkin' too, why you pickin' on me?" This would be the way it would go, day after day. Most times when I was trying to discipline the students, the teacher would notice that some sort of a contretemps was occurring, and would jump in to help me. Other times- for example when multiple groups of kids were having inappropriate conversations throughout the room- the teacher would ignore my difficulties and just try to shout over the hubbub. But either way, the entire concentration of the class was disrupted, and the teacher's lesson plan would fly off the rails. While I or the teacher was attempting to get one small area of the class under control, in another kids would be commenting on who in their immediate vicinity was passing gas, sneezing, or who had just had a fight with who, so a continual uproar engulfed us despite the best efforts of both the teacher and myself.

Getting the kids names right was serious business. Difficult though it was- remember I mentioned before, both the teachers and I were expected to recall the names of hundreds of students who rotated through our classrooms (and that those names were amazingly diverse and hard both to pronounce and remember)- if you forgot a student's name big consequences could result! For example the last year that I worked as a para, a teacher dealing with a misbehaving kid, who unfortunately couldn't remember the name of the wild boy, called him several different names while he steadfastly refused to give her a hint as to what his name actually was. Finally, in frustration, she said to him, "What if I say to you, okay black boy, just go sit over there?" She might as well have been the Japanese bombing Pearl Harbor! Such a hue and arose about this incident that you would have thought that someone had burned down the school. Within days the teacher, branded a racist by the entire community, was fired. This despite the fact that everyone felt absolutely free to call me a white man, and that the white students were identified as such by both their peers and the staff. In any case, I could see that every day tons of bad behavior was ignored by the adults in the building simply because they didn't want to be embarrassed by the fact that they couldn't remember the students names. Of course, the little monsters took full advantage of the adults' mental deficiencies. When substitute teachers were in or new paras were assigned, the troublemakers would make up names- they'd say: "I'm Ben Dover" or "Frank Furter" or even, "Les Befriends." When the sub would send referrals down to the principal's office with names like that, they'd become a laughingstock and would start to worry if they were ever going to be called back to substitute teach again. So, like I said, the easiest thing was usually just to pretend not to see the bad behavior.

The incivility that these kids manifested obviously had been passed on to them by the individuals laughably called their "parents." A good example was an Hispanic boy we'll call "Jose", who was notoriously rude and foul mouthed. Now, dear readers, many of you I am sure are taxpayers; please be aware that 85% of these children receive (thanks to you) free or very reduced priced lunches. In addition, since we all well know that their parents can't bother to make them breakfasts before school, despite the fact that their families are on food stamps, free breakfasts are provided to about 50% of them as well. I'm sure that more would participate in the breakfast program, but as they couldn't get themselves out of bed on time, many more who qualify unfortunately missed out. Jose, however, always seemed to make it down there. Now since Michelle Obama has been the first lady, the breakfast program has had an emphasis on providing the kids with nutritious foods such as fruits and vegetables and whole grain cereals despite the fact that our little monsters would prefer more sugary fare.

One morning Jose turned down the breakfast choices the little gray haired 65 year old cafeteria lady was providing him with and screamed at her, "Give me a fuckin' cookie!"

Shocked and incensed by his verbal abuse she turned to a friend of mine, the teacher supervising that morning (we'll call her "Mrs. Mazurka") stating that she was not only not going to give him a cookie but she thought Mrs. Mazurka should call the boy's mother and tell her what he said. At about ten o'clock she did and woke the groggy mother out of a sound sleep telling her that Jose had been so disrespectful that he hadn't been served and ended up missing breakfast. Now keep in mind that Jose was twelve, and his dead- to- the- world mother at 10 am (Jose did mention to us that she often would party all night) was only twenty-seven, so maybe Mrs. Mazurka maybe shouldn't have been so surprised when this "mother" shouted to her on the 'phone: "Why are you callin' me at this time of night? What the hell's the big deal? Just give him the mother fuckin' cookie and leave me out of it!" Then she slammed the 'phone down on the teacher's ear. I told Mrs. Mazurka that it was too bad that she couldn't have squeezed in a few words before the young lady had hung up, maybe she should have asked to speak to her parents? Possibly they would have understood what was so inappropriate about the boy's actions. Maybe not. Who knows? The teacher and I pondered long and hard as to how many generations we would have to go back in this family before we could find a civilized human being. Considering that Jose's family (and many of the other families of the kids in our school) came about from teenagers having children, I'm sure that Jose's great grandparents, if they're still alive, would be about my own age!

To give you an idea as to how adverse some of these so-called "parents" were to hearing from the school, one time one of the Hispanic paras that I worked with had numerous problems with a student that she had been working with. She had made many attempts to call the mother- always without any success. Usually the little rascal just chuckled about Sue's inability to get through, but after one particularly outrageous episode when he was really convinced that he might be suspended, he told her: "Miss Sue, call my ma on your personal cell phone 'cuz she doesn't know that number- she's got calls from the school's official number blocked!" Imagine if this child (or any of the many other children at the school whose parents pulled these kind of stunts) had gotten injured or became sick during the school day? How would we have gotten through to that household? In my opinion, some of these parents ought to be hauled up on charges of neglect!

8
How They Saw Me

Speaking of racism, sometimes I had my own problems with accusations of that. One girl, we'll call her "Nangeret" (Remember all the names of people and places in this narrative have been changed to protect the innocent, the guilty and to stymie the litigation-happy) became unhappy when I persistently forgot her name the first few days of school. When she asked me what my problem was, I explained that I wasn't used to all these modern names, and that when I was younger everyone had had easy names like "Bobby" or "Billy" or "Jane." "Mr. Shine", she shouted, "that's racist!" Try as I would to inform her that I was only stating a fact about my past, and that I wasn't trying to be racist, she stubbornly hung onto her bad impression of me and I had to apologize over and over again, and to back-pedal frantically as I was afraid that she'd report me to the administration. She was a spirited and intelligent young girl, and later she and I became good friends, but due to my inadvertent comment we obviously got off on the wrong foot!

Even with my co-workers crazy episodes occurred. I have never been a morning person, so it was kind of hard for me to get to school for 7:30 am.

I liked getting there promptly though, as I loved listening to the kids on the PA system, as they'd recite the Pledge of Allegiance. I was happy to hear the kids say it – it was the one time - when God would be mentioned at the school. Believe me, I sorely noticed his absence the rest of the day! Anyways- not being a morning person like I said, I was certainly in no mood for "lunch" at 10:30 am. When I'd go to our break room then, I was shocked to find the Hispanic paras coming in with heaping trays of food that they carried up from the cafeteria: turkey dinners with all the trimmings, meatballs swimming in sauce with piles of spaghetti, fried chicken with gravy, mashed potatoes and corn. I couldn't imagine people eating like that so early in the morning at a time when I really thought of it as breakfast, so I'd shake my head in disbelief. The co-workers would eye me suspiciously eating my tiny, little sandwich that my wife had brown-bagged for me, and they'd say, "Mr. Shine, is that all you're eating?" They could see from my considerable girth that I was a big eater so, of course, they questioned. I'd come back with, "I can't believe you people can eat like that...." (I was going to say, if they had let me finish "so early in the morning") but they'd all shouted in unison "YOU PEOPLE, YOU PEOPLE, WHAT DO YOU MEAN BY YOU PEOPLE! ARE YOU TRYING TO SAY SOMETHING ABOUT HISPANICS?" I'd stutter and stammer and try to explain that I wasn't talking about their nationality, and that I'd only meant that I couldn't understand how "morning people" could eat in such a hearty manner so early in the day, but nothing I said could seem to get me out of the verbal hole I had dug. There'd be much nodding and winking among them, and then they'd revert to speaking in Spanish and I'm quite positive that nothing I said was convincing them that I wasn't a racist! Which was really kind of sad. I know, dear readers, that right now you're asking if I want a little cheese with my whine, but the fact that so many people just assumed that I was a racist really cut me to the core. When I was a teenager myself, back in the 60's you see, I had been an early follower and admirer of Doctor Martin Luther King. As a matter of fact, my family and friends, back in those days, used to call me a "nigger-lover." I even signed up for what was called "The War on Poverty' and when Doctor King was assassinated I had been volunteering to work at a community rec. center in the ghetto. On the actual day of his assassination, my mother warned me not to go to work, as I had explained to her that I had the only white face there. Being, even then, a conscientious soul, I insisted on going to work anyways, and found myself literally following Christ's teachings of "turning the other cheek" as I was battered and slapped by quite a few of the black male teenagers who shrieked that I was a "honkie." Eventually, some of my black co-worker counselors (who had stepped in to shield me from the worst attacks) insisted that I go home for my own safety- which I then did. So you can imagine how hurt I was that now the children and grandchildren of the generation that I had volunteered to work with still were having these misconceptions about me! It's a funny thing about life, as the years go along, what was wrong becomes right and what was right becomes wrong.

9

The Mechanics of the Place

Each classroom had a panic button. When the teacher, or the para, would push the button after a long, long period of time the principal might come in. By this time the class was in a total uproar. It usually took the principal about twenty or twenty-five minutes to respond to the panic button but, at that point, when the principal finally walked into the room and the kids saw the principal's face, they would all fall totally silent. They all would remain so during the following five minutes while the principal would scream and yell that he (or she) was going to suspend the entire classroom, call their parents, take away their privileges etc. etc. But, as soon as the principal left, within five minutes the classroom would return to it's previous level of chaos! If the principal didn't show up all we could do was to try and cope the best we could and hope that the forty-five minute period would soon be over. I remember occasions like that when forty-five minutes could seem like forty-five hours!

Students who misbehaved were sent to the principal's office with what the kids called "right ups." The official school department's name for these was "Referral for Disciplinary Action" slips. Although they were primarily filled out by the teachers we paras too could submit them if a child's behavior was becoming totally out of control. Offences that could result in referral ranged all the way from assault, possession of weapons or drugs, on down to less serious matters such as insubordination or disruption to learning. The first year I worked in the district over 18,000 of these referrals were issued, but by the time I retired three years later, the number had declined to "only" 14,000. We have approximately 18,000 students in my city so you might be tempted to think that each student received one referral or so per year. But that's not the way at all that it went! Some kids, the chronic trouble-makers, would get forty or fifty referrals a year while the great majority of the students, those we probably would have called back in the 60's or 70's the "forgotten, silent majority" seldom got any. I often wondered why the parents of these poor kids who constituted the forgotten, silent majority didn't sue the school system because of their children's inability to receive an education due to the fact that they had to sit in classrooms with these disruptive troublemakers. Or maybe, even better, they should have sued the parents of the disruptive kids whose uncontrolled spawn were blocking the silent majority's opportunity to learn.

Students sent to the principal's office with write-ups faced wildly varying consequences. One principal we had, call him "Mr. Hueggins", would often just give the kid a lollypop (he kept a big barrel of them on his desk) and send the offending child back to class. This ineffectual authority figure, who retired with a $100,000 pension in his mid-fifties while I was working at Williams, was rumored to have hidden under his desk when little girls only four feet high had gotten into a slap fight in his office! He was the one who used to walk up and down the hallways shouting at the students every morning with a bullhorn, demanding that they hurry up to their classes. When he left he took his bullhorn with him. I hope it was his personal property and that it didn't belong to the school.

The other principals, who at least tried to be a little sterner than Hueggins, would give the written-up child a tongue lashing or warning before sending the kid back on to class. Warnings were the most common result of referrals to the principal but for more egregious offences (like assault or fighting, destroying public property etc.) suspensions would occur. The authorities tried to stay away from out-of-school suspensions as the theory was that "a student not coming to school was unable to learn" so in-school suspensions were greatly preferred.

Children who had an in house suspension, the day after the offense, had to go to the in-house suspension room. This was a small, windowless room that was supposed to be a quiet study-hall type area where the kids were expected to do their schoolwork in absolute silence. As usual with Williams, nothing worked they way it was supposed to!

Of all the teachers in the school, the one I felt most sorry for was Mr. Rodrigo, the one who had to supervise in-house. Instead of sitting quietly the kids would argue constantly, throw things at one another (and Mr. Rodrigo) and jump around like monkeys. He pushed his panic button ten times a day but as the miscreants assigned to his care came from all three "houses", as they were called at the school, it was unclear which principal should come up to help him. In 99% of the cases nobody came at all, so all he could do was to tear his hair out and scream all day long. Kids who had gotten into fights with one another the previous day, had to sit side-by-side with their enemies in the small room, so the fights of the earlier day were often re-ignited. Luckily for Mr. Rodrigo, the in house room was adjacent to the school library and friendly Mr. Peru, the school librarian, would help Mr. Rodrigo out by pulling the most obnoxious students out of in house and would let them spend the day in the library. There, they happily would spend their time either surfing the Internet, or talking to their friends, so it turned out that in house wasn't such a bad place after all! At least for the kids. As far as Mr. Rodrigo fared, it wasn't so good for him. Although he was a young man, he confided in me that he had developed high blood pressure and a serious nervous disorder.

But, like I said, the kids didn't really seem to mind it much. Sometimes they even wanted to go there voluntarily! I remember one little girl, Jasmine, who would run up to me many a morning and say, "Mr. Shine, look I'm out of dress code (half the kids in the school were on any given day), send me to the principal so's I can go to in-house!" She wanted to go down there because she knew most of her friends would be there and she wanted to hang out with them. Other times, a student might want to go there to avoid a teacher than they didn't like or to miss a class that they found to be distasteful.

A much more effective punishment was after-school detention. This, unfortunately, was seldom used for two reasons: one, the offending student would often just jump on the after-school bus and not show up and, two; teachers never wanted to volunteer to stay after-hours to supervise the behavior- challenged students. This was despite the fact that the teachers were offered overtime if they would agree to stay in the detention room to baby-sit the little monsters for an hour or so. We paras, who filled in for the teachers throughout the school day, were, for some reason, deemed to be unqualified for the detention- babysitting role and were never offered the job. As a result, to my chagrin, after school detentions were only scheduled one or two times per academic semester!

Although it went against the establishment's druthers, the principals were forced to implement out-of-school suspensions for students who had committed the most egregious offenses. But these too were of limited usefulness. The trouble-making kids who got them, as I mentioned before, often came back to the classroom waving their out-of-school suspension paperwork like badges of honor, and these wild ones looked upon time off from school as a fun vacation anyways! The most time, no matter how badly they had behaved, they could legally be suspended was ten days, but such long suspensions were unusual, one to two day suspensions were generally the norm.

Another reason why the out-of-school suspensions accomplished so little was the fact that they had no effect whatsoever on the child academically. The teachers would "ask" the suspended child, on their return, to make up tests or projects that they had missed while they were suspended but that was purely voluntary on the teacher's part. Instead, the educators were forced to count only the marks the kid had gotten while he was in school- totally ignoring the massive amounts of work that he had missed while he was suspended. That's why (together with William's generous "social promotion" policy) kids who had had as many as thirty-five or forty out-of-school suspensions in one academic year, kids who had only actually been in school only ninety-five days out of a one hundred and eighty day school year, could be promoted to the next grade! The kids knew the system better than we did so they knew everything that we were doing was just a joke, they were going to be promoted anyway, that we had no leverage.

Many teachers, in disgust, just stopped writing referrals at all. They told me, "Mr. Shine, what's the point? I write the kids up and nothing's accomplished. So why bother?" I'm sure that's the reason the amount of referrals decreased 20% in my district during the three years I worked there. It's certainly not because the kids behavior improved by 20%! I know that the higher ups in the administration were very proud of the fact that referrals had decreased but I think, instead, that a lot of the teachers were just giving up. A fair amount of the teachers just tried to handle whatever problems came up by themselves with mixed results.

Sometimes, students who had brought large amounts of drugs to school or who had seriously injured other students or caught carrying weapons, were "arrested."

I put the word "arrested" in quotation marks as the charade the police went though with these monster kids really, in my humble opinion, was not a real arrest per se. Yes, the policeman involved would take the child out in handcuffs, and yes, they would take the offender down to the police station, but then the scoundrel would simply be released into their parent's custody, and five or ten days later the kid would be back in school as if nothing had ever happened! Of course their name would never be published in the newspaper and jail time never accrued. As a result of these escapades probation officers would sometimes be assigned to these delinquents, and sometimes these probation officers would even stop by the principal's office to see how their charges were doing, but I and the other paras would often snicker when that would happen, as we knew that not much was going to change with such hard cases. We felt sorry for the parents of these kids who frequently confided to us that they were unable to control their offspring. These parents, some of whom suffered beatings at the hands of these "youth", were fated to be stuck with these soon-to-be criminal kids. Just as we were. Being one of America's 100,000 public schools we had no control over whom we had to admit and over who would be walking our halls. As Clint Eastwood would have said, we were saddled with "The good, the bad and the ugly." As I am sure that the reader has already guessed, the kids with probation officers would brag about that fact to the other students. In some ways Williams was like a correctional facility on a smaller scale, the "badder" you were, the better it was for your "cred."

Williams had three or four school counselors who were always busy. Their offices were generally filled to the breaking point with the worst of the troublemakers who were allowed to go and see them whenever they wanted. As so many of our students had fractured home lives and myriad personal problems, especially revolving around their inability to deal with a structured environment such as school, we probably could have benefited from three or four times as many! Some of the counselors just followed Mr. Hueggins' example of passing out lollypops and candy, and the kids would kind of just hang out in their offices playing games and skipping their classes. Some of these counselor's offices were adjacent to the library so kids would kill time in the library all day surfing the 'net and talking to friends while they supposedly were "waiting to see" the counselor. As they were trying to bull their classes they would ignore the fact that the counselor didn't seem to be around (sometimes he might even be off for the day!) and few bothered to try and shoo them back to their classes, because when you did, it was like stirring up a hornet's nest. A few of the counselors though, for example a flamboyant black man named Mr. Haynes who dressed like a hip-hop star, did seem to have some good talk therapy skills. He, I know for a fact, defused many a brewing fight and de-escalated many a volatile situation. The kids admired and respected him and thought he was "cool"- we could have definitely used a few more like him. Still, what the counselors could accomplish, even Mr. Haynes, was extremely limited. Students would be good at the counselor's office because all they did there was "rap' about various subjects and play games- it was rare for this better behavior to be carried over to the classroom where the student was actually supposed to be doing some work, or learning something! I too, could get along fine with the kids if I just allowed them to play around in class, or talk among themselves. It was only when we asked them to do a little work that all hell broke loose. Troublemakers who had three or more maximum ten- day out of school suspensions in one semester (a two and a half month period) were given a "Manifestation." More students than you might think were possible needed these. No, a "Manifestation" was not some sort of medieval exorcism of evil, but was rather a big PPT (Parent, Pupil, Teacher) meeting where the educational team would get together with the offending student and his parents to try and determine what should be done to break the cycle of disruptive behavior. Usually some big shot well paid, mucky-muck from the downtown central office that didn't know the student or his parents at all came down to run the meeting. This expert from the special ed. department usually had the greatest input as to the solution that the team implemented. During my tenure, possibly due to my out-spoken nature, I was only invited to sit in on one manifestation session although the other Paras frequently were. Of course, being Hispanic, they also functioned as translators for the experts from the central office as they spoke to the kids' parents. The most common "solution" that the team would come up with from these meetings was to place the malefactor into a different academic house. The theory apparently was that if you took the student away from his group of friends and placed him with another bunch of kids that he would start to behave better. Sometimes this actually worked (at least for a short amount of time) but mostly it just served to inflict the crazy kid's antics onto a larger number of previously unaffected fellow classmates. Another tactic frequently employed were behavior sheets that the student would have to have each of his teachers fill out and bring home for his parents' perusal, or one to one Para assignments so that he (or she) would be shadowed by a Para all day long to personally supervise their behavior. The behavior sheets to be brought home didn't usually work half as well as the administration would have liked-I specifically remember one student who used to rip them up and throw them into the garbage each afternoon right in front of me rather than bring them home! And as far as shadowing the student one to one went, that too was problematical. Shadowing the worst bad apples was one of my main assignments at Williams and, I must say, due to the fact that I was never allowed to put duct tape over the mouths of any students, I never really was able to prevent any of them from disrupting their classes. I did, however, jump in and physically restrain some of them from assaulting their fellow classmates, so I suppose I did some good after all!

> So the wild ones continued in their wild ways despite the use of the techniques mentioned above, but for those who had multiple manifestations in one year, the heavy artillery had to be called out. Technically a really horribly disruptive kid could be permanently expelled (as opposed to just suspended) from the school system, but in my years I never saw that happen. The mantra of "total inclusion" espoused by the administration prevented that from ever occurring!

> Instead, the two biggest cannons that the administration had when it came to dealing with the recalcitrant student were to either one, place him or her into one of our district's two alternative schools, or, two; send them to BDLC. The alternative schools, one of which was the State Street School and the other one was called the "Enlightenment Academy" (the central office seemed to love euphemisms) took difficult kids in from throughout the district and treated them more in a quasi-military, boot-camp like environment. The staff at these schools had the freedom to use some innovative methods and their results sometimes were surprising! As far as BDLC goes, BDLC stands for "Behavior Disorder Learning Center."
>   Every year when I went back to work at Williams that's where I feared being assigned most. Although I didn't want to quit my job I told my wife that if they ever assigned me there I was going to quit! BDLC was in a separate area of Williams where all the rottenest apples were rounded up and any staff assigned to it always was trying to transfer out. Luckily for me, I never actually was placed there. Maybe the administration knew that I'd quit if I had even gotten wind of such a thing.

The way BDLC worked was that the students (who were supposed to be kept basically segregated from the main population of the school), were kept for hours on end in separate classrooms by the sternest teachers they could find. Although chaos still reined in those classes as well, when I first arrived at Williams, BDLC teachers had the ability to send their worst problems to a classroom called "the quiet room." This was a windowless, almost furniture less room similar to in-house. Here the student could scream their lungs out but they weren't allowed to leave. A big burly teacher or para stood at the door and physically restrained the child from leaving for a specified time period. This system, backward as it may seem to you dear reader, seemed to have a salutary effect on the behavior of these difficult children, and made BDLC at least somewhat manageable for the staff. Unfortunately, the second year I was at Williams, a big controversy erupted in a small city twenty miles down the line from us about the use of these "quiet rooms" in the public school system. The whole controversy played out in the media as civil rights advocates called the use of such rooms inhumane so our administration, ever adverse to bad publicity, told our principal to stop letting the teachers and paras physically stop the wild kids from walking out of the punishment room. Instead they were instructed to just follow the kid as he walked up and down the hallways of the school, or wandered into classrooms (or often the library) at will. Well, at least they were right there if the kid decided to assault somebody! Of course, morale among the staff in BDLC hit a new low.

Since nothing at Williams ever worked exactly the way in was supposed to, the BDLC children were really not kept entirely segregated from the general population. They were allowed to sit in (and disrupt) the ADL (Activities of Daily Living) classes every afternoon with the rest of the kids. The theory apparently was that these classes like music, health, sewing, and gym etc. were less rigorous than the academic classes in the morning, as well as being more interesting, so hopefully, the BDLC kids would behave better in these classrooms. Again, this theory only worked out occasionally. One good thing though, was that the BDLC students had paras with them to quickly escort them out of the ADL classes whenever they would start their rambunctious behavior. The fact that the teachers (and the silent majority children) in these classes had to endure these distractions never entered into the equation from the Administration's point of view. Our higher-ups worshipped at the altar of "inclusion" and the needs of the teachers and the silent majority of the students, who seemed to really want to learn these subjects, basically could be ignored!

I think that even the staunchest advocates of the cocky-mammy hypothesis that "there's no such thing as a bad child" soon began to realize that it wasn't a good idea to have the worst culprits in the school wandering around the place all the time -terrorizing the helpless, younger children so, the last year I was there, they had the quiet room (at some great expense) out-fitted with cushions and pillows. They piped in soothing music and, using semantics, changed its name to "the meditation room" and BDLC teachers and paras were now told that they should "encourage" misbehaving students to stay there. What the staff was supposed to do if one of the students forcibly wanted to leave was left unclear. The higher-ups sent mixed messages. If the kid was physically restrained that was considered a no-no, and yet if they let the child escape and go wandering the halls at will, that also would draw a reprimand. Morale hit yet another new low. When Lori, a para friend of mine, asked our principal Mr. Ripello, how she should square this circle he told her, "Maybe, sometimes it might be good to take more bathroom breaks." With crystal-clear directions like this you can imagine with what fear and trepidation she faced each year's performance evaluation. I think you can understand now why it was that I always dreaded being assigned to BDLC!

From the wild child's point of view, however, BDLC could have one big advantage; kids whose behavior was really egregious and who gave the staff enough of a headache, would often be allowed to come to school for time-shortened days. Dismissals as early as eleven-thirty or noontime (essentially a half-day schedule) were often permitted. So, the haters of school, even if they were sent to BDLC, found themselves winning another victory; they hated school intensely and now, because they had made themselves obnoxious enough, they were rewarded by having to attend less of it! Like I said before, we really had very little leverage over these kids, no matter what their behavior was, and worst of all; they knew it.

10
Why They are the Way They Are

I'm sure that you're asking yourself by now, what in heck was wrong with these kids? Why are they so different from my fellow students back in the halcyon days of my youth, and, more importantly, why are they so different (in a negative way) from the millions of other kids in America's better performing schools?

Well, they suffered from a plethora of problems that we didn't know about back when I was young. Or, if those problems were known about, they only seemed to affect a small number of kids (most of whom were institutionalized in those days) instead of the whopping percentages of the student populations that are hobbling the educational environment in our modern schools. For example, we had a large contingent of autistic kids wandering our halls. "Kids" is probably a misnomer. Some of these "kids" were six feet tall or higher and often could tip the scale at two hundred pounds or more! Although they were usually closely shadowed by a para or an individual called a behavioral specialist (who was paid ten dollars an hour more than normal para due to the difficulty of the work), they often had violent tantrums or fits when they would attack themselves or others. The last year I worked at Williams there were twenty-eight attacks by these autistic kids on staff that resulted in workman's compensation claims against the city and extended medical leaves. And that's not taking into account all the attacks they inflicted on the other kids. Nobody ever kept track of those statistics!

But far more common were students with A.D.D. (Attention Deficit Disorder) and its subcategory A.D.H.D (Attention Deficit Hyperactivity Disorder). The two syndromes overlap and kids diagnosed with one of these were usually diagnosed with the other as well. Although neither of these maladies was recognized (or even known to exist) back when I was going to school they have been accepted as legitimate and verifiable psychiatric disorders of childhood and adolescence by the D.S.M (Diagnostic and Statistical Manual of Mental Disorders) since at least 1994. Wow! I've got clothes in my closet older than that! Symptoms of these disorders in children include:

- Are easily distracted, miss details and frequently switch from one activity to another.
- Have difficulty maintaining a focus on task.
- Become bored with a task after only a few minutes.
- Have difficulty focusing attention, organizing or completing tasks or learning something new. Trouble with completing and turning in assignments or homework, often losing things (such as pencils or papers) needed to do mandatory work.
- Do not listen when spoken to.
- Daydream, become easily confused and have a hard time following directions.
- Fidget and squirm constantly in their seats while talking non-stop.
- Dashing around, constantly in motion, touching or playing with everything in sight.
- Very inpatient, have difficulty doing quiet tasks or activities.
- Frequently blurt out inappropriate comments and show their emotions without restraint, having no regard for the consequences or the feelings of others.
- Extreme difficulty waiting for things they want, unable to wait their turn in classroom activities or in games.

It is a matter of enormous controversy as to how often these "disorders" occur in children and exactly what percentage of students are afflicted. In the United Kingdom, where a strict diagnostic model is followed, less than 1% of their kids are adjudged to be suffering with these syndromes, whereas here in the U.S. approximately 10% of our children supposedly are impacted. In schools like Williams where our country's achievement gap is most evident, kids with these and other, what are called "behavior learning disorders" can easily constitute 20-25% of the classroom population! I can attest to that figure, as I generally had to mentor and supervise six or seven, what we paras called "special ed. kids", in every thirty to thirty-five student classroom. Needless to say, unless an exceptional teacher was present, that high a percentage of behaviorally and learning- disabled kids in a classroom often was enough to make learning an impossibility for the mainstream students stuck in those rooms. That this was happening, and it might actually have anything to do with the achievement gap that everyone in the educational system was lamenting, wasn't something that anyone in the administration ever worried about. Our higher-ups were all far to busy worshipping at their altar of inclusion to ever worry about such a common sense problem!

Here in the U.S., the most common treatment for these maladies revolves around medicating the child. The drugs generally used are Ritalin, Adderall and Dexedrine, with other similar mood-changing meds frequently prescribed as well. Although child psychologists tell us that these medications do a good job of ameliorating the symptoms enumerated, and my fellow paras often blamed episodes of misbehavior on kids not taking their meds that day, I really couldn't see that much of an improvement in the craziest kids behavior whether they took these drugs or not. In other words their behavior was SO EXTREME that I could hardly believe that it would have been any worse had they dumped all their meds in the trash. Take their meds though they did; I remember on the one occasion when I got to go on a field trip with Mrs. Rosneff's class to the science center, we had to bring along many paper bags filled with the kids' various medications. Just as an aside, I might want to also mention, that we had to bring along paper bags filled with inhalers too, as unfortunately 30-40% of these inner-city kids suffered from asthma! What we as a nation are doing to our kids is really something that should be examined.

Studies claim, that left untreated, A.D.D. and A.D.H.D in childhood and adolescence can lead to anxiety and mood disorders, together with sexual promiscuity and substance abuse issues in adulthood- hence the rationale to medicate. But the more I studied about these bug-a-boos of modern childhood the more confused I became!

Going online I found out that hundreds of studies have indicated that many of the behavior problems that cause kids to be diagnosed with these disorders can be lessened by letting the kids participate in vigorous physical activity. I thought back to when I was a kid that age. We had recess!

James W. Shine

When I was young we'd come running in from recess and we'd be so pooped that we'd gladly sit in our chairs and listen to the teachers. Now, in our middle schools we have no recess. Young teenagers bursting with health and vitality are told to sit in their seats quietly, for hour after hour, at a time in life when their hormones are exploding, and their animal spirits are forcing them to bounce off the walls. No wonder even the "normal" kids have a hard time concentrating! Yes, we still have gym, but the way that works will probably surprise you readers. Now (at least at Williams) they would send 50-60 kids down to the gym at a time for a forty-five minute period. There were far too many kids there at once for any meaningful teams to be formed and many kids just sat on the sidelines. If you just showed up the gym teacher (who always wore a whistle around his neck) would put down that you passed. Sporadically a kid would get a chance to kick a ball on a twenty or thirty person team, or a smaller more athletically inclined group would have a vigorous basketball game; but we never got a chance to go outside and run around the school track or in any way get all the students involved. Most kids would come back from gym without ever having worked up a sweat, and often returned punching each other and play fighting, tickling on the stairwells and hallways; as they had gotten just enough physical activity down there to stimulate their hyper-activity thresholds, but not enough to satiate them!

Another important, often over-looked factor in the whole ADD/ADHD debate is the role nutrition (or the lack of good nutrition) plays in instigating these behaviors. I, as well as I'm sure anyone who has worked with kids, could easily see what happened when they consumed too much sugar. It became hyperactivity city! So I wasn't surprised when I read online that thousands of studies (some at Harvard, Cornell and Oxford) found that up to 76% of the children with these diagnoses could experience dramatic improvements in their behavior with improvements in their daily diet! What miracles of modern education we could probably implement if we could just get these kids to stay away from excess sugar, food additives, and to eat a decent breakfast.

Doing a little research of the web, I came across an interesting book, "Mental Health: Not all in the Mind-Really a Matter of Cellular Biochemistry" by Chris Meletis and Jason Barker. In this literature a study by Jennifer Dani, Courtney Burrill and Barbara Adams found that: "The result of this analysis is that nutrition has potent effects on brain function. It concluded that protein, iron, iodine, and the consumption of breakfast all impact on a child's learning capability and behavior. Moreover, recent research has identified additional, potent roles of micronutrients, such as essential fatty acids, minerals, and vitamins, in the prevention of learning and behavioral disorders. Among, the latter, this review focuses particularly on attention deficit hyperactivity disorder."

I therefore wasn't really surprised to find that most of the kids (especially my behaviorally challenged assigned cases) were gorging themselves all day long with salty, sugary snacks that they carried around in their backpacks. Sadly to say, although all the staff at the school intuitively knew of the potential of "sugar shock" to worsen the hyperactivity problems, many of the teachers would wheel carts filled with snacks like these from room to room. They would sell this junk to the kids to raise money for field trips and special activities. They would also "make a party" in their classrooms on an almost weekly basis during which they'd ply the students with baked goods and cookies in order to bribe them into better behavior or as a reward for a couple of days without any horrific incidents. Nobody ever seemed to worry much about how these sugar- shocked dynamos were going to behave in the following class! Many of my fellow paras too, passed out candy on a daily basis. They'd tell me, "Mr. Shine, we don't have any problem with these kids, there always good for us. Maybe you should pass out candy too." I suppose bribery is often effective, but, on the other hand, I thought to myself, "How can these hyped up, sugar shocked kids, be able to sit in their seats and concentrate?" Besides, I knew that someday these students were going to go out into the big bad world out there, and then there wouldn't be anyone sitting by their side, bribing them moment- by- moment into barely adequate behavior! So, I didn't pass out the candy.

While researching this book, I also became aware of the findings of University of Delaware psychologist Brad Wolgast. Wolgast found that many students who think that they have attention deficit hyperactivity disorder are actually often just sleep-deprived! Doctor Wolgast said, "Whenever you find depression, anxiety and hyper-activity in students, when you scratch the surface 80 to 90 percent of the time you find a sleep problem as well." He went on to opine, that simple steps to improve what he called, "sleep hygiene," are usually far preferable to prescribing drugs like Ritalin or Adderall (whose side effects we shall mention shortly). The good doctor's findings didn't surprise me at all, as I recalled that most of my ADD and ADHD kids would never cease to brag that they had often stayed up until the wee hours of the morning posting on their facebook pages, yapping on their cell phones, or watching TV! That these young technology obsessed youth were sleep-deprived couldn't be doubted in the least bit. Trying to give them advice about getting a good night's sleep seemed to be nothing but a waste of time, and they proudly told me that their parents never forced them to turn off their gadgets and go to sleep at a reasonable hour to prepare for school the next day. It was then that I began to realize that just as in farming, that preparing the field properly was just as important as the seeds that were sown, so also, in the educational field preparing the child's mind and body properly (basically the job of the home and the parents) was just as important as the work done by the teachers once the kids arrived! I think that today, many of us have forgotten this fact. In our rush to implement teacher "accountability" we are more than ready to penalize many fine teachers because of their lack of results when, through no fault of their own, they have been assigned classrooms of kids unable to listen. After all, do we pull the license of a dentist who advises our child to floss every day- and then the child doesn't follow his advice? Is it fair then to take away a teacher's livelihood when their advice too has fallen on deaf ears?

Another interesting aspect of ADHD is the factor that age, vis-à-vis the child's classmates, plays in its diagnosis. Doctor Helga Zoega, a fellow at the Mount Sinai School of Medicine stated, "The youngest kids in the class are often diagnosed with ADHD." Backing this up, a Canadian study done of 12,000 boys between the ages of six and twelve found that the youngest cohort of boys were much more likely to be diagnosed with ADHD (7.4%) versus the oldest cohort (5.7%). Another study of seven to fourteen year olds, found that the youngest third of the children in the study were 50% MORE LIKELY in each grade level to be diagnosed with ADHD than their grade mates who were chronologically in the oldest third! It begs the question, are ADD and ADHD just the modern way of describing what we would have called, back in my day, simply "immaturity?"

And, it's not as if the drugs that we employ to mask the symptoms of ADD and ADHD are not without serious side effects! Among these side effects are (according to the DSM):

- Growth suppression
- Increased risk of developing Bi-Polar disorder

- Increased risk of developing mood disorders
- Increased risk of causing serious psychiatric episodes
- Increased risk of developing sleep disorders
- Many children may become addicted to these drugs.

As many as 10% of this school-aged population is assumed by pediatricians to have what are called "addictive personalities" so use of these drugs as a crutch can, and often will, lead to the use of illegal drug substances (and even alcoholism) as an unfortunate consequence for these students in later life. So, you have to ask yourself, are we really doing these kids a favor forcing them onto these medications? I've got my doubts!

The etiology (causation) of these maladies is also something that gives scientists pause. Unlike unquestioned diseases that stem from genetic defects, like Downs Syndrome, ADD and ADHD seem to spring out of the child's social milieu rather than having anything to do with the child's biological or genetic makeup. Wikipedia states, "Children from certain backgrounds are much more likely to be diagnosed with ADHD. Among frequent predictive factors we often find single parent family status, parental divorce, large family size and young age of the mother." Following along with this, Wikipedia throws out the statistic that up to 18% of all the children of alcoholic parents will be diagnosed with ADHD, so it would seem that the BEHAVIOR OF THE PARENTS has something to do with the development OF THE SYNDROME IN THE CHILD! Could that be the reason that noted psychiatrist, professor and scholar Thomas Szasz said, "ADHD was not discovered, it was invented!"

Completely agreeing with Professor Szasz is the noted child pediatrician and researcher, Doctor Michael Anderson. Doctor Anderson gave an interview to the New York Times on Oct. 9, 2012 (which you can read for yourselves in their Online edition) in which he stated that ADHD is a "made-up disorder" and is being used as an "excuse" by the educational establishment for their failure to properly educate the vast majority of our special ed. kids.

Although he obviously feels guilty prescribing powerful drugs like Alderall to the poor, unfortunate youth brought to him by their parents at the demand of the schools, he stated in this interview that, "I don't have a choice to prescribe or not to prescribe." He continued, "Because we as a society have determined that it's too expensive to modify the kid's environment now we as pediatricians are being forced to modify the kid." Doctor Ramesh Ragavan, a close colleague of Doctor Anderson's went on to say, in a similar vein, "We as a society have been unwilling to invest in very effective non- pharmaceutical interventions for these children and their families. So we are effectively forcing community psychiatrists to use the only tool at their disposal, which is psychotropic medication." Both doctors feel that they, and most of the other pediatricians in America, are being pushed into using powerful, potentially harmful drugs on children in an often futile attempt to boost poor academic performance in woefully inadequate, under-performing schools. Humm... Kind of what I've been saying!

11

Maybe this is Why They are the Way They Are

Maybe the doctors and the studies that I quoted have nothing to teach us, maybe our LD (learning disabled) kids should just keep popping their pills like good little robots as the educational establishment wants, despite cases like Richard Fee's where Alderall use has proven to be fatal, but you know, I've got a different take on this whole child behavior problem. Possibly there's a different causation going on here! Let's take a look again at the kind of behaviors these classroom- smashing youngsters present. They:

- Are easily distracted, miss details and constantly switch activities.
- Have a hard time focusing on a task.
- Have difficulty focusing attention, organizing, completing tasks, or learning new things. Have trouble completing and turning in assignments or homework. Often lose pencils and papers.
- Do not listen when they are spoken to.
- Daydream, are easily confused and have a hard time with directions.
- Fidget and squirm constantly in their seats while talking non-stop.
- Dash around, are constantly in motion touching everything.
- Are inpatient, have difficulty doing quiet activities.
- Frequently blurt out inappropriate comments and show emotions without restraint, have no regard for consequences of their actions or the feelings of others.
- Have extreme difficulty waiting for the things that they want, unable to wait their turn in the classroom or while playing games.

What would we have called those kinds of behaviors back in my day? We would have said, as I stated before, that these kinds of behaviors were evidences of IMMATURITY. We would have said that what we were seeing in these children were CHARACTER FLAWS. We would have put much of the blame on the fact that certain kids displayed these character faults on the NEGLIGENT PARENTING skills of their parents! But were we wrong back then? Instead, are these learning disabling traits really the result of the quasi-medical conditions that our modern educrats posit?

As this entire book is basically coming to you dear readers as "dispatches from the front lines" of the educational quagmire here in our inner cities I'd like, at this point, to quote from a letter to the editor of our city's local paper. The letter was written by a Mr. Shane Dufresne, a distinguished police officer who had just retired after working in our district's schools and simultaneously in the department's youth division for more than twenty years. He wrote:

"One thing many people gloss over is the home situation and parental involvement in their children's development. I know one factor may not make or break it, but this is a strong one.

Over the years, we have blamed superintendents and teachers for lackluster student achievement. We have had new superintendents and new, energetic teachers because of retirements. Yet student test scores barely budged. How about putting the blame where it belongs: on the students and their parents?

During the last three years on our city's police department, I was assigned to the Youth Division. Part of my duty was to visit every grammar school at least once a week to lend support to the staff, serve as a role model for the students and to talk to kids who were headed down the wrong path. Yes, there were quite a few on that path in this age group.

One parent told me she would not let her children do homework. She said teachers have the kids for six hours a day, and at home is their time. One parent said she didn't have time to help her children with their homework. A few months later, she and her boyfriend were charged with running a drug factory out of their house.

I was asked by one principal to sit in on a meeting where the mother had threatened to assault a teacher if her son was held back again. She was yelling and swearing as she entered the school and did an about-face when I emerged from the principal's office. Some parents encouraged their children to fight other children and staff if they felt threatened.

During visits to student's homes with principals, I have found children with soiled and dirty clothes and shoes that didn't fit, and children who looked and smelled as if they hadn't showered in a week. Some of the homes were filthy.

Then, when we filed reports with the state Department of Children and Families, we were the bad guys to the kids and parents, though a few appreciated our help.

I have friends and relatives who are educators in this city. They say they spend half their time disciplining students and taking time away from those who want to learn. This problem is easy to solve: TAKE ALL DEFIANT AND HABITUALLY TROUBLED CHILDREN OUT OF THE CLASSROOM, AND PUT THEM IN ISOLATED CLASSROOMS OR IN SEPARATE SCHOOLS altogether until their problems are addressed and they can get the help they need. Then put them back in class. The problem with this is that groups such as the American Civil Liberties Union would say that this is a cruel and unusual punishment, that they are being singled out unfairly, and have a right to be in their class. No, they don't, not if they are CONSTANTLY DISRUPTING THE CLASS AND THOSE WHO DO WANT TO LEARN.

Sadly, this won't happen. Knowing the system, we will continue to blame teachers and future superintendents. We will still be scratching our heads and wondering what's wrong.

I guess it's easier to blame a superintendent or some teachers than to hold thousands of students and their parents accountable. The problem is we'll keep going around in a circle, and the kids will be the losers in the long run. "

But is this just one sourpuss' opinion? Well, in addition to me agreeing with him, Judy Ball a retired teacher from our city's school system, apparently agrees with him too; as she too also wrote a letter to the editor stating:

"Municipalities and school systems continue to address issues of discipline that have a negative impact on student learning; dilute the amount of time available to administrators to observe and support staff; and cost taxpayers money.

Unfortunately, we have allowed a society to develop in which basic constructs that once encouraged positive life habits are disappearing. Family strength, respect, work ethic and shame all have powerful roles in producing our young. How can these be restored?

It is necessary to stop rewarding those individuals who do not work, do not act responsibly and exist by literally stealing their lifestyle from hard-working people who follow the rules.

The needs of those who cannot fend for themselves must be met. However, until the government demands active labor participation for public assistance; until young women cease to be rewarded financially for wanton reproduction; UNTIL PARENTS LEARN TO BE PARENTS; and until people learn the well is going dry; the problems in our schools will continue.

By the time a child is in middle or high school, he or she may be beyond salvage-although in some cases, with the support of a caring staff member, a child can be rescued.

It behooves us to look to the decision makers who set in stone our social policies. IT MANDATES THE MODELING OF TRADITIONAL VALUES FOR OUR LITTLE ONES.

Mayors and first selectmen, educators and board of education members; your position is unenviable. As you fight to allow learning to transpire for those who want to learn, you can be compared with the boy who put his finger in the dike to hold back the sea. EVENTUALLY, THE HOLE WILL GET BIGGER. Then what does one do"?

This NEGLIGENT PARENTING'S effects, although they often produced little monsters which neither I, nor the rest of William's staff could control, sometimes had heart-wrenching consequences as well. Remember Ms. Brenner? The excellent teacher I was talking about a few chapters ago? She told me the story of a small hellion of a boy, eleven years old, who was constantly fighting with the other kids, and continually defiant towards her. He was the very epitome of a little ghetto tough guy, a gangsta wanna-be; a kid she had to send to the principal's office (and I remember this part well) almost every other day. One day, she said, he began blubbering and crying uncontrollably in her class, carrying on like a two year old. Why? She kept a tickler file with her class roster, and she knew it was his birthday. So she stuck a little candle in a cupcake and gave it to him while singing the "Happy Birthday" song. That's when the crying jag meltdown had begun! "Mrs. Brenner", Myquan said, "ain't nobody ever done given me no birthday party befo." I wasn't there when this happened, but she told me that he had continued to sob throughout almost the entire rest of the class!

12
Glimmers of Hope

Despite the fact that the "No child left behind" act had mandated that, by 2014 100% of the kids in America would reach proficiency in Math and reading, today in my city as we approach that year, only 39% of the students were even scoring at grade level on the standardized tests! And, it's not exactly as if this act has been under-funded. So far, as a nation, we have spent 25 BILLION on this program. Spending on education, in constant dollars, has TRIPLED in the last forty years while, meanwhile, SAT scores in 2012 hit a four- decade low and the average reading score is down 34 points in the same period! Eighty-two percent of the high school graduates in my district needed remedial classes during their first year of college, and our true high school graduation rate was only about 60%, if we look at it from kindergarten to graduation day, as we should do. Instead, to play with numbers, the city counted the percentage of eight graders who made it out in four years. That way they could bogusly claim a 68% graduation rate!

What has been the "educational blob's" (as John Stossel calls them) response to all these indications of failure? Simple. Unable to reach the goals, forty-seven states (including mine) applied for, and received, waivers to the "No child left behind act." Oh well, if you can't cut the mustard just apply for a waiver!

Now the latest thing I heard is that my state government may be stepping in to take over and run some of the worst performing schools in our district. I guess the theory is that what the smaller bureaucracy can't do, the bigger bureaucracy will be sure to succeed with. Again, I have my doubts, as my northeastern state hasn't balanced a budget in years, is ranked dead last in business friendliness, and is number one in per-capita debt per taxpayer, I'm sure they'll do a fine job running my city's school system! Yeah, and there's a bridge in Brooklyn I want to sell you too.

Be all this as it may, as the years pasted gently by at Williams, my opinions slowly began to undergo a sea change. As I got used to the cacophony echoing in the halls, I started to realize that what I was really hearing was the high spirits, higher energy, and the boundless enthusiasm of youth! It slowly soaked into my obsolete, technologically challenged brain that, all in all, THIS WAS A HAPPY PLACE! Like an old man suddenly forced to drive in a high-speed demolition derby, my initial observations had been somewhat clouded by my initial anger and, in all honesty, by my instincts for self- preservation. As the academic years followed one another and my eyes incrementally adapted to the darkness of today's inner-city educational system, I could see that there was every bit as much joy here as there had been in the schools of my youth. Maybe there wasn't as much learning, but there was just as much happiness!

Once I began to stop worrying about getting popped by the wildest students (or having spitballs thrown at my head) I started to notice all the twelve-year old girls skipping down the hallways hand in hand. I noticed the clumps of boys; the natural high-spirited mini clusters of adolescent males, "chillin" together as they play fought and laughed every day. In their exuberance they'd leap up, like kangaroos, and whack the "exit" signs above the doors! The twelve and thirteen year old girls like girls of that age everywhere, loved to scream. In the enclosed, windowless stairwells going down to the cafeteria, how'd they'd shriek at the top of their voices! They'd laugh and laugh. The more I'd jam my fingers into my ears, the funnier they'd think it was! And the louder they would get! Yeah, I can't deny, Williams was basically a happy place. Now, as I'm retired and finishing this book of my observations, I find myself kind of missing all the energy and boundless youthful happiness I found there.

I realized, as all successful workers with children and teenagers do, that these kids had just too much energy for us to demand that they all behave like little robots twenty-four, seven. Instead, I learned that you had to practice a bit of triage and let a lot harmless baloney pass by, while cracking down on the truly egregious behavior.

Another thing about Williams that I was thrilled about is that many (although certainly not all) of the students had progressed towards the post- racial acceptance that we want to see in modern America. There was no "West

Side Story" type of animosity of blacks against Hispanics as I had initially feared might be a problem when I first took the job. Instead all the kids got along really well, and accepted the various races and ethnic groups, probably, at least in my mind, a tad sight better than their parents would! Even the true minority, the white kids, wasn't picked on either. Of course, I think that it helped that those white kids like M&M, adopted the ebonic speech patterns, clothing styles, and mannerisms of the dominant black and Hispanic culture. As I mentioned before, the only kids that really were looked down on were those "nerds" who liked to study! And even they were seldom actually physically attacked but instead were only scoffed at. Many of the kids did seem to feel that white people were racist (especially older ones such as myself) but they didn't project that racism towards the young white kids in their own age group.

Another thing that I noticed is that, when they wanted to, these kids were really quite capable of learning. An example of this is that they all coughed into the inside bends of their elbows! I know that I'm probably dating myself, but when I was young I (and everybody else back then) would cough (or sneeze) onto the outside of our closed, upraised, fists. Being an older individual, I still do that today. But children now-a- days have all been taught by their teachers, I suppose from kindergarten on, that they're supposed to cough or sneeze into the inside bends of their elbows. And, you know what? THEY ALL DO! Even the biggest, wildest, troublemakers that I dealt with all practiced this new (to me) more hygienic way of masking our coughs or sneezes. So, I began to think about it, if we can teach kids on a universal basis such a simple thing, who knows; maybe we could teach them to respect their elders, the value of hard work, and a million other life-changing lesions!

Speaking about respecting your elders, for those of you readers overflowing with schadenfreude and who think that the problems that I've been addressing in this book don't affect you, as your kids don't go to inner-city schools; there's no doubt in my mind that all of us in America, city dwellers and suburbanites alike; have been doing a terrible job of imparting decent moral values to our children.

Among the things that made me think this was the infamous case of Karen Klein, the sixty-eight year old bus monitor, who was bullied and mocked to tears, and whose video became an Internet sensation. In this horrible incident middle school students told her, "You don't have a family because they all killed themselves because they didn't want to be near you." They also said to her, "Stabbing you would be tough, because you're so damned fat." I took a lot of abuse from the kids too, but never quite that bad! Luckily for Mrs. Klein, one of the nicer students on her bus posted the video on "You tube", where it went viral and sympathetic viewers raised three quarters of a million dollars so this fine lady could retire. I, on the other hand, had to endure months and years of abuse for not much more than the minimum wage! But the important fact to take away here is that the Karen Klein case happened IN THE SUBURBS! Mrs. Klein worked as a bus monitor in Greece, NY, which is not an inner city at all. So, like I said, the disrespect for older people, the wild behavior, are certainly not confined to the inner city schools that I originally began writing about.

All over the country, in city and suburb alike, the chaos in our public schools continues to worsen. Just for an example, in 2012 Theresa Reel a New York high school teacher, was awarded a $450,000 settlement for being nearly raped in a classroom. Or, we could look at the case of Bailey O'Neill, the twelve- year old boy who died in 2013 as a result of a beating inflicted on him in the schoolyard of a middle school in Darby Township, Delaware, another SUBURBAN venue!

Nevertheless, as the school years followed each other, I started to see, albeit haltingly, a few incremental changes for the better. The second year I was at Williams, Doctor Padula (by the way I'm going back to changing names after having quoted research works and verbatim cases taken straight from recent headlines) was promoted to principal of our adjoining high school and was replaced by Mr. Ripello. As I stated before, this gentleman at least seemed to have a more realistic understanding of the problems we were facing.

Among the first changes Mr. Ripello made was to change the bell schedule. He staggered the class periods so that all the periods didn't start and end at the same time, doing this accomplished a major change, the biggest kids- the eighth graders, weren't running around the hallways at the same time as the tiny sixth graders! The hallways became a little less chaotic, and we had fewer instances of the little ones being trampled by schoolmates as large as their parents. He also expanded, and insisted that we teachers and paras follow, the PAWS (Positive Attitudes Working Safely) program. Although at first this program seemed silly, once it got up and running it did produce some positive results. The way it worked was that whenever staff observed one of the kids doing something good- whether sharing with another student, taking turns nicely in class, helping collect supplies etc.- we'd give them a bright red ticket with their name on it. The ticket said, "You have been caught displaying PAWS pride! Congratulations"! Students loved getting these tickets, and when they got them, they'd bring them down and place them in a drum in each house principal's office. He'd then hold frequent drawings to determine which kids would get various prizes. Obviously, the more tickets the child garnered, the more chances they would have to win a prize. Every week, each house principal called out scores of names and gave out tons of prizes. Most of the prizes were just candy bars or certificates for pizza, but the kids really seemed to love hearing their names called out over the loudspeaker, and soon they were competing to get these PAWS tickets! Any behavior modification expert will tell you that positive reinforcement is far more powerful than the stick - at least in most cases-and I (and the other paras) soon found that by carrying around and doling out these tickets, we could influence the kids' behaviors for the better. The students would clamor for them, and by threatening to withhold a PAWS ticket, or contra wise, promising to bestow one; we could sometimes ratchet the classroom environment towards something where actual learning became possible! I used the tickets on a daily basis; the way I looked at it, passing them out was like passing out candy- without the sugar shock drawbacks.

The second half of my three- year stint at Williams benefited from some other fortuitous headwinds. The Police Athletic League (PAL) in my city was totally revitalized, and massively expanded, by a very active, and youth friendly, police chief who later went on to become mayor. Mayor O'Looney built youth community rec. centers for the kids and enrollment in PAL went from just a few dozen to seven or eight hundred! More police mentoring was happening in the inner city and little by little, as greater and greater numbers of my students participated in the various athletic teams sponsored by PAL, or had help with their homework from the police volunteers down at the rec. centers, attitudes of the youth towards the police began to change drastically for the better! These improved attitudes carried over (at least somewhat) towards the way the kids interacted with their teachers and the rest of us in authority. The violently anti-police and anti-authority outbursts mentioned earlier in this book-thankfully- became substantially less frequent.

Throughout this chapter I have been talking about things that have given me "glimmers of hope." But in my last year at Williams I encountered something far more than a glimmer- I encountered an entire searchlight beacon- a blinding sun of hope that was SO BLINDING and SO TRANSFORMING that, for a few days, I actually was tempted to throw this entire book into the garbage and move on to something else! This game-changing revelation was not some new program, or some new educational system. No. It was something much simpler; I was lucky enough to meet a very special teacher!

Ms. Stango, whose name I am not changing as I'm sure that she'd approve everything that I'm going to say about her, was a young, white woman in her late twenties or early thirties. I've mentioned good teachers in this work before but, even compared to them, Ms. Stango stood out like a brand new shiny diamond ring in a box of raisonettes! During the last six months of my stint at Williams I was privileged to be assigned to her and was totally flabbergasted at what I observed. I thought that I had been magically teleported to one of the finest schools in the country! THERE WERE ABSOLUTELY NO DISTURBANCES, wild behavior or any other kind of shenanigans! It was truly an eerie feeling to be standing in her class at 8:15 and hear nothing but the cadence of her voice and the scratching of the student's pens and pencils, while through the cinderblock walls I could hear (and feel) the chaos and din from the surrounding classes! She closed her door to block out the jet-plane roar of the hallway and, like I said, her room was an oasis of quiet and calm in that impossible place. She taught 7th grade English and she taught it well, not dumbing it down, but rather challenging her students to give it their all, and to work to the best of their abilities. Every one of her students worked fine for her and gave it their very best. I never, EVER, heard anyone talk back to her and cross talk among the kids themselves was at an absolute minimum and seldom disrupted her lesson plans.

At first I found it quite mysterious that she could tame these wild beasts so completely, accomplishing something that the rest of us, lamentably, were so inept at. But, as the weeks and months went on, and I studied her methods closely, I began to put my finger on the pulse of some of her secrets. In the hopes that some teachers (or students studying to be teachers) are reading this narrative, I am now going to describe her methods and mannerisms in some detail.

One's first impression, in the classroom at least, of Ms. Stango was that she was a mechanical woman. She spoke in a clipped manner and moved about the room in a kind of herky-jerky way that left a body wondering if she was a flesh and blood human being at all. She kind of reminded of you of a robot teacher!

Ms. Stango never raised her voice, or lowered it either, but rather spoke in a sort of lulling monotone that was quite comforting to hear, and might even be described as hypnotic. I never heard her hollering or yelling at any student, but neither did she whisper. She was absolutely, totally, unflappably. No kid could ever get a "rise" out of her or could seem to change her composure in any way! She bulldozed through her lesson plans like a force of nature, and never joked with the kids or tried to be friendly as other teachers frequently tried to do. She also never brought herself down to the students' silly level (as most of the other teachers often did), but instead stayed up on her robot teacher, unflappable God-like pedestal; and you know what? The kids seemed to like it that she was up there!

She had a strange way of speaking. Every thing she said was very complex, and you had to listen very carefully to understand her. As she didn't raise her voice, and what she was saying was so complicated, the room of necessity had to be very quiet, and you had to concentrate with all your brain- power to get what she was saying. From her there were never any two -word outbursts towards the kids like the rest of us used. You'd never hear her bellowing at the kids; "Shut up" or "Be quiet" as we paras and the rest of the teachers did all day long. Instead she might say in her clipped rapid manner something like: "Alright students, it is now 8:05 and we are going to begin reading chapter seven, 'The use of Pronouns', we will begin with the row of desks by the door, and going down the row every third student and each will read one paragraph. We will begin with you, Jasnell." Like the other good teacher Mrs. Brenner that I mentioned before, she had a way of making the students feel foolish and guilty if they couldn't follow her complicated instructions, and like Mrs. Brenner also, she was able to get the other students in the class to start scoffing and laughing at the daydreaming kid who was unable to keep up! Kids didn't like to be laughed at by their classmates, and she soon had each child concentrating with their fullest abilities and hanging on to her every word. Because they had to pay such close attention to what she was saying they were unable to fool around or bicker with one another. Needless to say, I had little to do in her classroom!

How did she handle disruptions? As I mentioned before, she never yelled at students; rather she reasoned with them. If a student began whispering in her class she might say something like, "Mr. Hurdle as you obviously feel that what you have to say is so important that it should take precedence over today's lesson plan, maybe you should go to Mr.Yeshiva's office and explain to him why your ruminations should be incorporated in this school's curriculum." The whispering kid, probably only half understanding what she was saying, would get embarrassed, turn red in the face, and start to stutter. The other children would start to laugh and, as you can imagine, he never would ever whisper in her class again! As a matter of fact, her increasingly difficult directions and spiraling upward expectations of the students, kind of became like the old school game we played when I was young called "Simon says." And, just as in that game, the kids paid closer and closer attention to her each class period as the minutes wore on.

Day after day I was amazed by her classroom management abilities and the fact that the students, for her at least, were learning so well and so thoroughly. I never had to remove a child from her class and had only to walk up and down the rows trying to give a little extra help to the special ed. kids that she had in there. The competition to keep up and to do well in her class became so powerful that surprisingly, many of them would shoo me away and say, "Go away Mr. Shine, I got this myself!" Or, "Go away and help somebody else Mr. Shine, I've got this now!" While in other classes these "special" students weren't shy about using their learning disabilities as excuses, in her class nobody wanted to be seen that way. As I said she brought out the absolute best in all her kids

Each day when she and I parted company I would say to her, "Every day you show us that it can be done." She would just smile her modest smile. Other times I would suggest that she might want to spend some time mentoring the other teachers. But she never responded to that. Among the other teachers Ms. Stango maintained a humble, self-effacing persona. I, and the other paras, found it very puzzling (and somewhat disingenuous), that when we had staff workshops where teaching techniques were to be taught to the teachers, teachers whose classroom management skills were totally non-existent, were the first to get up and bloviate, while teachers like Ms Stango would just sit quietly and say nothing at all! I suppose she's just not the kind of person who's very good at blowing her own horn in a bureaucratic setting. That's too bad, because her methods are the type of methods that the other teachers should emulate. Unfortunately, when she was out (which- by the way she seldom was), and I was alone with her class, or if a sub was filling in for her, the kids would immediately revert to their usual impossible ways. This, of course, was the proof that what she was doing, SHE WAS DOING, and that it wasn't because any special "cherry picked" group of kids were assigned to her. But the fact was- that she did what she did! She completely controlled, dominated and successfully taught a classroom full of rambunctious, wild inner city kids! And, knowing that my experience is limited, I'm sure that she's NOT THE ONLY TEACHER DOING WHAT SHE'S DOING! Ms. Stango helped me to realize that although being a successful inner city teacher is a very hard job, it's not, by definition, an impossible one! It can be successfully accomplished! As I said, she didn't give me just a glimmer of hope, she showed me a beacon, she showed me a spotlight!

Finally, for reasons that I'm going to outline in the next chapter, the census at Williams began to fall. Instead of the 1500 students that we had when I first arrived, significantly fewer kids were being assigned to us and the other middle schools in our city. With one or two hundred less bodies to contend with, the hallways became a little less crowded, and the classes got a little smaller and more manageable! The staff seemed to have a little better handle on things and the kids' outrageous behaviors became not quite so severe. Williams still was the Wild West, but it felt like its heyday had passed, and that we were slowly moving towards more civilized times.

13

What My City is Doing

My northeastern state has the worst achievement gap in the country. My city, the fifth largest in the State in terms of population, had, as I mentioned before, twenty-one out of twenty-nine of its schools listed as "failing" under the "No Child left Behind Act." That something drastic needed to be done with our schools, both on a State-wide, and City-wide basis; was something that was constantly being discussed and worked on during the time I was at Williams and also during the ensuing year since I left.

The first thing that my city did, as we always seem to do when we have an issue here in America; was to throw money at the problem. Between 2005 and 2013 we embarked on a $284 million dollar construction program! Two entirely new schools were constructed, and seven other schools that were considered to be out-dated and maybe even somewhat dilapidated, were totally renovated and given new additions. Much of this program had to do with the shift from the middle school concept to the K-8 school model. This is an improvement, by the way, that I agree with 100%!

Middle schools are an idea whose time has gone. If we look back to their creation, back in the 1960's, we can see that they came about when the baby boomers' kids came along and began bursting the old elementary school system at the seems. They were originally meant to be a temporary, stopgap measure, a place to warehouse kids until some new schools could be built. They replaced the neighborhood schools that the students could often walk or ride their bikes to with enormous industrial-like education factories where (like at Williams) 1500 kids got packed in and everybody got lost in the shuffle! A gargantuan middle school complex is nothing but a bureaucratic nightmare where, as I mentioned before, half the time the staff doesn't even know your child's name and where your frightened kid scurries madly, dashing around from class to class, trying not to lose their books and just survive the day without getting beaten up or bullied. In most cases, your child is only a number and not a name! The kids themselves know this. They too hate the middle schools. If you read the best-selling book (which has now been extended to an entire series), "Diary of a Wimpy Kid" by Jeff Kinney you'll see on Page 9 where Greg, the protagonist, says, "Middle school is the dumbest idea ever invented. You got kids like me that haven't hit their growth spurt yet mixed in with gorillas who need to shave three times a day." AMEN and once again, AMEN!!! Enormous amounts of educational time are wasted every day (perhaps as much as 20% of usable teaching time) as the children wander the hallways constantly between the 45 minute periods, always packing up and settling down, while losing pens, papers and books. I suggested that maybe it would be better if the teachers rotated from room to room, but of course, no one ever listened to me.

In stark contrast to these failing educational factories, we have the beloved old neighborhood school. These schools are now being extended to go up to grade eight so as to totally eliminate the failed middle school concept.

Among the greatest advantages of the K-8 system is that, as in all the elementary schools, you have one teacher, all day, in one classroom of 25-30 kids. This teacher (and the para for the class) gets to know these children well, usually meets and has some type of relationship with their parents, and soon learns the student's strengths and weaknesses. Of course, all the problems that we've been mentioning in this book aren't all going to be mitigated simply by going back to our old, tried and true elementary school method; and we did, in my city, have nearly a score of failing elementary schools, but, at least you're working with a model wherein the teacher and the child know each other! Another equally important point is that the staff is gaining access to the child when they're still young enough, and pliable enough, for their attitudes and behavior to be moldable. As Felicia Moore, the mother of a bullied daughter and author of the book "Children, Sing Along And Learn With Me", said, "You can't wait until they're teens to reach out to kids, then they think they know everything and it's too late." Boy, is she ever right! Kids who were so dumb that they had to pull the waistbands out of their underwear and check, so they wouldn't misspell the word "fruit", daily confronted me, who's spent more than sixty years on this planet and probably worked at more different types of jobs than their entire families combined; with dismissive "know it all" attitudes that made me sick to my stomach. These are sixth graders that I'm talking about! I'm sure, though, that back when they were little kindergarteners even the ones from totally dysfunctional families were much more amenable to adult supervision, and would show more respect for their teachers and other staff. Just being with the students from those tender years so that the kids "grow up" with the staff has to be an enormous advantage over the educational- factory middle school concept, where thousands of swaggering pre-teen monsters meet scores of teachers and paras with whom they have no history! From everything I've been told, the seventh and eighth graders going on with their education in the new K-8 schools, and who are continuing with the staff that they've known since kindergarten, were presenting only a fraction of the discipline problems that we were seeing in the middle schools. Of course at Williams (and I'm sure every other humungous middle school throughout the country), the administration futilely attempted to recreate the manageability of the old neighborhood school by breaking the students up into "houses" or "groups", like the "red" group, or the "blue" group; but these lame concoctions succeeded no more than the King's effort to put Humpty Dumbty back together again. Children would constantly try and figure out where their group stood in the pecking order and would frequently ask, "Mr. Shine, I'm in the 'Blue' group, is that better than the 'Orange' group?" The teachers held almost daily conferences, and kids would be shuffled in and out of these groups at a blinding pace, but despite all the turmoil involved nothing was successful in recapturing the intimacy, and the one on one child to teacher contact, that the kids missed so much from their elementary school days. In any case, as the "feeder" elementary schools for Williams were slowly being converted into the K-8 format, the sixth grade introductory classes coming in got smaller and smaller, so our middle school's census (and that of all the other middle schools in our district) fell sharply while I was there, and while I was writing this book. We went from 1500 kids to less than 1300 and, all in all, that's certainly a good thing!

Another thing my city did was to begin construction of a second high-school level vocational school. Our existing vocational school always had three or four times as many kids applying for spots there than were available. So, building a second vocational school is definitely going to help! Not all kids are cut out for the academic path, and one thing we surely have to do is to get over the mantra, in this country, that "everyone has to go to college." As a matter of fact, a report from the Center for College Affordability and Productivity found, using figures from the 2010 census, that despite graduating with student loans averaging $28,000, 48% of all working college alumni (not just recent graduates) were either totally unemployed or were underemployed. The vast majorities were working at jobs in retail, sales, or in other less than professional positions that they easily could have qualified for without any postsecondary education at all! So what's the big deal about college? Better to be a well paid plumber than to be a college graduate Starbuck's barista! Our kids, even our inner-city kids, intrinsically know this and bitterly resent the way we try so hard to push them to learn all sorts of academic things, many of which, they haven't the slightest interest in. They feel like failures when they can't correctly conjugate verbs or remember tidbits of history when, instead, they could be feeling like successes working with their hands as carpenters, electricians, or beauticians!

The very "misfits" who seemed so hopelessly inept in their academic classes (possibly because they had no interest in them) could demonstrate a blinding intelligence in other aspects of life where they obviously had a greater interest. To give you an example, we had a young with- it teacher, call him Mr. Swatz, who came in one day with the very latest combination cellphone-computer tablet gadget. This gizmo could surf the 'net, take pictures, download videos and even upload the student's test scores and completed homework assignments to Williams' mainframe computer. Our twenty- something teacher loved it and was showing it off to the class, but began complaining bitterly how expensive it was to pay for all of his "apps." "Mr. Swatz", hollered out Deldar from the back of the room. Now Deldar was a major behavior problem and was far from academically gifted; as a matter of fact he ended up being suspended 36 times that school year. "Mr. Swatz, let me see dat thing, I think I can fix your problem." Deldar fiddled with the tablet for less than five minutes, smiled and handed it back to the young teacher. "Mr. Swatz", he said as he beamed, "I 'jailbroke' it for you, you gonna have all your apps now and you ain't gonna hafta pay a thing." You could have knocked Mr. Swatz (and me) over with a feather! He still had all of his apps, but Deldar had managed to free his gadget's connection to all his expensive providers! This is just one example of the kind of thing I witnessed day after day. These kids didn't know what a past participle was, they most likely didn't want to know, but they were veritable whizzes when it came to computers or any kind of new technology.

Think of how much they could learn if we were teaching them what they want to know!

But my city's nearly $300 million dollar school building and renovation program that, in a six -year period, remodeled more than a third of our buildings, wasn't the only thing they did. Just putting up new buildings (and remodeling the old ones) creating more shining palaces of stupidity where the same old failed methods of dysfunction and failure are enshrined is of limited value. John Stossel, who writes about as cogently as anyone on the subject of our modern educational failures wrote in one of his columns. "Los Angeles spent half a billion dollars to build the most expensive school in America. The school system planted palm trees, put in a swimming pool and spent thousands of new dollars per student. The school is beautiful, the education? Not so good. The school graduates just 56 percent of its students." Luckily for us beleaguered taxpayers in my run-down northeastern city they didn't insist on planting any palm trees in the new schools, although they did put in some swimming pools and each building featured soaring foyers and acres of plate glass! Nevertheless, I'm happy to say that others (beside myself) slowly, as the years of failure went on, realized that METHODS HAD TO BE CHANGED as well as bricks and mortar.

One great idea that they came up with the second year I was at Williams was something called the "Academy." The administration culled out a hundred or so of the best kids, both academically and behavior-wise, coming into the school in their first year in sixth grade and put them in dedicated classrooms separated from all the other chowder-head, yeh-who population. They called this "school within a school" the "Academy." If these students continued to deserve it by their progress and behavior, they remained in the academy throughout seventh and eighth grades as well. The academy kids were kept totally segregated from the general school's student body, they even ate their lunches at separate tables and passed through the hallways at different times than the rest of the students. I suppose that the administration did this so that the good academy kids wouldn't get "infected" with the wild, disrespectful behavior so epidemic throughout the rest of the school. I know, we here in America today are in love with the idea of "inclusion". We are all great believers in it and are certain that it's the solution to all of our problems. But you know what? I hate to tell you this; but when it came to the academy, it was obvious to me, SEGREGATION WORKED! Whenever Mrs. Levessure at the academy asked me to watch a class for her, I found myself in an oasis of calm and quiet where learning was going on at a far faster pace- without all the ridiculous disruptions I was used to-and the small amount of time I spent there was a true pleasure. Each and every class at the academy functioned (whatever the skill level of the teacher who happened to be in there) at the level of standards that I had observed in Ms. Stango's class. In other words, extraordinary, award-winning teachers weren't absolutely necessary in that setting as the children themselves were thirsty for knowledge and had no interest in turning their classrooms into circus venues. I know, logically, that every student can't be in the academy but, if I had a child (or a grandchild) who had to attend Williams, I'd want him or her to be in the academy!

Another great idea that they had was something called the "Arts Magnet School."

At a cost of a hundred million dollars or so, seventy percent of which was paid for by the State, my city built a soaring, sparkling-new cathedral of education in the middle of our downtown that was closely connected to a branch of our State University. Although at first, as a taxpayer, I was skeptical of spending so much money, this turned out to be one of the best investments that we ever made! This school, which was a kind of Charter School (we'll be speaking more about these in the next couple of chapters), set aside forty percent of its seats for kids from the suburbs. The administration handpicked music, art, and technology teachers who had histories of superior rapport with students from middle school age on, and turned them loose to teach subjects that the kids were not only interested in, but were crazy about! As the university was right next-door, professors and college students could often pop over and help with the classes. The kids at the Arts Magnet School took classes in video production, computers and their softwear, theater, rock'n'roll music, marketing and technology. Just as with the vocational schools, four or five times as many kids wanted to get into the spaces set aside for our city's children, so lotteries had to be set up to allocate the openings! Be that as it may, discipline problems at the magnet school were non-existent and the testing results from the kids there soon began to elevate the scores for our entire district, which is something that really pleased the educrats downtown. Of course, it goes without saying, that any boy or girl with any sort of behavioral problem whatsoever had no chance of being admitted there; so the teachers did have the advantage of working with the best of the best! I would have loved to work at the magnet school but I had no such luck, my skills were relegated to working with the kids where more heavy lifting was necessary.

I had mentioned before that many, many of my students frittered away their nights, up until the wee hours of the morning, blabbering on the cellphones, listening to hip-hop music, incessantly checking their facebook posts or viewing porn on the web. The cold light of dawn (when school promptly began) found them good for shit. As far as being capable of being able to learn anything at that time? Forget it! As a matter of fact, as a para, it was one of my jobs to gently prod snoozing students during their early morning naps so their snoring wouldn't disturb their fellow scholars. Belatedly recognizing this problem my city, starting in 2013 at a cost of $875,000, began a program whereby a 180 of these types of night owl kids could begin going to school from 2 pm to 7 pm as opposed to having to deal with the regular early-morning school day. Children were chosen for this afternoon, early evening school setting if they had been frequently truant, tardy or had displayed behavioral or social problems. The night school kids benefited from smaller ten to fifteen student classrooms, and counselors were on duty to help them "talk through" any issues that they might have, whether about home life or the school environment. According to our city's new special education supervisor, in addition to the academic curriculum, frequent classroom discussions on these issues would be held as well. Well hallelujah! It's about time! Although I feel that the city could put a zero on the back of that number of the kids chosen to participate in this new program, at least it's a start. Progress usually comes in small ways, and yes, this, and the magnet school may just be baby steps; but they are good steps nevertheless and at least are indications that we were making a good start to work on our problems.

During the years I was at Williams a big technological breakthrough came along as well, and this also turned out to be a major game changer. What I'm talking about is the invention of what is called the "Smart board." These high tech devices cost the city $14,000 apiece and were gradually installed into every classroom in both our school and throughout the city. The Smart Boards replaced the old-style chalkboards or white boards at the front of every class with an enormous computerized device connected to the teacher's desktop computer and visible to every kid in the room. The Smart Boards used "Word" and our young generation of teachers, who are all crazy about computers, were soon typing madly into them, posting all the class notes, math problems and so on! They were even able to post all kinds of pictures, diagrams and videos on the screens and as they had a "touch screen" interactive feature, the kids were able to come up to the front of the room and work with the Smart Boards directly. As the kids loved computers too, they were very eager to come up and work with them. The same children who languished in the back of the room, and never volunteered to come up before when we had chalkboards, couldn't wait to rush up front and work with the Smart Boards whenever they got the chance! Kids loved them so much that they would try to sneak into empty classrooms just so that they could play with them. The staff had to keep an eye out for that as they could then, inadvertently, mess up the Smart Board's delicate settings. Most of the teachers, and this was the board's greatest benefit, began making the students copy much of their information off of the smart boards instead of using all of those insufferable handouts that I had complained about earlier in this book. This not only cut down on all the mess in the classroom but it elevated the learning curve astronomically! As I mentioned before, when the kids got handouts they often just glanced at them and threw them away, but when they had to WRITE THE MATERIAL it was passing into their brains using their motor neurons too. As one special ed. teacher told me, when it came to working with special ed. children, "We read it, we say it, and then we write it. Using three senses, we have three times the chances to get it stored into our brain!" This is so true. Kids learn so much better when they copy. I suppose the teachers could have had the students copy from the old fashioned chalkboards, and some of them did, but many of them didn't seem to like writing much with chalk (maybe they didn't like getting chalk all over their hands and their fine new clothes) so I noticed that student copying increased dramatically once the new Smart Boards came in. And, like I said, that was a good thing.

The academic administrative class (educrats) who came up with all of these programs didn't always bat a thousand though. Maybe because most of them hadn't actually taught in a classroom any time in the last ten years, their well-meaning innovative concepts sometimes didn't bear all of the fruit that had been hoped for. Despite the fact that each and every one of these educrats pulled in salaries of $125,000 a year plus for a nine month a year, six hour a day job (well they did have to sometimes attend evening meetings), disappointments were known to happen anyways.

An example of this happening is what happened with the "Gear-Up" program. Our city was lucky enough to snag an eleven million dollar grant from the US Department of Education to participate in this potentially very positive experiment. Called "Gear-Up", as in "Gear Up for success" this new program was designed to provide mentoring in academic, social skills and self-esteem together with after-school lessons in Math, Science and English. Individualized attention was going to be given to the "at risk" student participants in Gear Up right through high school and into college. This excellent opportunity was eventually offered to all the seventh and eighth graders in our city (except those in the magnet school already) and six hundred slots were opened up. What happened? Only three hundred kids signed on. Like I said- a bit of a letdown! But I wasn't completely surprised.

When I worked with the kids I couldn't help noticing that laziness was a major problem. They didn't want to take advantage of opportunities provided to them whether it was in the form of extra help, one-to-one tutoring, or whatever else was offered. When I could see that they were goofing off, I'd holler at them to "Do your best." They'd answer me "Mr. Shine I am doing my best!" but all the while, they were writing one-word answers or doodling on their papers. I'd then shoot back with, "Listen, you can lie to me- that's alright. You can lie to your teachers and your parents, it's not good, but you've probably been getting away with it for years anyways, so it's no big deal. But when you start lying to yourself it's really getting bad!" If looks could kill, I'd be dead, but it brought to mind an old saying that my old Irish father used to say whenever I disappointed him. I know that it's not politically- correct any more now-a-days but here it goes: " You can fix a lot of things, but you can't fix stupid. You can cure a lot of things, but you can't cure lazy!" Unfortunately for us in this country, many of the kids that I was working with were both STUPID and LAZY. Some of you readers now may be getting angry, but I'm afraid I have to call a spade a spade, and let the chips fall where they may. Anyways, like I was saying the Gear-Up program, at least in my city, never lived up to it's wonderful potential.

The children in my city's public schools (and Williams was quite reflective of this) were 75% black or Hispanic. In the earlier chapters I implied that with some exceptions, like Ms. Stango and Ms. Brenner, the children seemed to relate better to teachers of their own ethnicity. Despite this fact, 88% of our district's teachers were white, while only 12% were minorities! My fellow paras were almost invariably black or Hispanic, as were the cafeteria help and the maintenance workers. Why not the teachers? It's not like that teachers weren't well paid. In my city their salaries averaged $63,000 per year and the union just negotiated a six percent raise over the next two years. So why weren't more minorities being hired?

The mucky-mucks in the central office apparently also realized, possibly maybe prompted by the parent neighborhood school groups that had been complaining for years, that this was an issue. So at a cost of $100,000 a year plus they created a new position called "Professional Development Coordinator." This newly-hired bureaucrat was charged with the task of going to black colleges and functioning as a recruiter for the city, he or she was also charged with the task of advertising our staff vacancies in Spanish language and other minority publications. Despite these laudable efforts, as of this writing, little progress towards recruiting more minority teachers into our system has been made. The main reason for this, I suppose, is the fact that percentage-wise there are, on an absolute basis, so few minority teachers. According to figures from my State's teachers colleges, the latest statistics indicate that only 9% of the 3,554 of the teachers graduating last year were members of a minority! Why is this? Aram Ayalon, a professor in our State's University Department of Teacher Education, when interviewed on this subject, claims that the expense of becoming a teacher may be a factor. Due to the student teaching requirement imposed and other issues, close to five years of college (or non-paid work) have to be endured before a teacher gets certified. In addition, Ayalon mentioned, then there's the MISTAKEN IMPRESSION that teaching doesn't provide a good salary. This together with the fact that many minority students have had a bad experience their first time through the public school system, gives many young minority college students pause before plunging back into the gristmill that tore them up the first time! As Professor Ayalon put it, "Why would you want to go into a profession, in a place you didn't like to be?" So true. Our State University system, together with my city, did have a program whereby we paras could get a couple of years of further education and then get certified as teachers, and I knew some paras who participated in that, but this wasn't foolproof either. Almost all of the paras were black or Hispanic so the program did have the potential of producing more minority teachers, but unfortunately, many of the paras working at the inner-city schools became so disillusioned with the system that they gave up on the idea of a career in education altogether! Anyways, when I think back to what teachers like Ms. Brenner and Ms. Stango are accomplishing, and I remember the fact that I saw many minority teachers treated like doormats by the students, I'm not sure that just upping the percentage of minority teachers in the school would be any sort of panacea. Much of the improvement in the educational process that I witnessed during my three years at Williams was, like the "Smart board" due to technological innovation. These innovations were spread out into all the thirty something schools that we had in our city. In addition to the "Smart boards" something called "Progress Book" came along. Each teacher, in every school, was given an e-mail address and was mandated to log in daily to the school's mainframe computer system. In addition to posting the class attendance information to the home office through the computer, all homework assignments, grades and test scores, and student's up-coming assignments were posted there as well. Parents, from home, could log onto the system and find out exactly how their kid was doing in every class, if they had done their homework, if assignments were due and so on! This turned out to be an enormous help for those conscientious parents who were diligently trying to monitor their child's progress, but of course was nothing but a waste of computer memory for those slacker students who could have given a hoot less about their education and those slacker individuals (loosely called "parents") who had brought them into the world and who had so ill-formed their ideas!

In an attempt to address the issue of the enormous amount of educational time wasted every day with the interminable fooling around in the hallways between classes, together with the set-up and breakdown period within each class, the administration, after contentious negotiations with the teachers' union managed to tack on an additional two days to the school year. This new school year period (182) days will be put into effect starting next year. Of course this can't hurt. Speaking about the teachers' union, they pretty much shot down what would have, in my opinion, been the most important reform for our school system of all!

First, a little background. I think that I've mentioned before that one of the most fortuitous things helping my city and its educational system was the election of a young, vibrate mayor who had previously been our police chief. As the police chief, Mayor O'Looney had totally revitalized PAL and expanded it to serve up to nine hundred young people, most of whom were living in our city's most blighted areas. Mayor O'Looney loved working with kids and, before he became Mayor, served on the City's Board of Education. Unlike his predecessor, he sat in on all the Board of Ed's meetings even after he was elected as Mayor. So he was well aware of what was the biggest problem in our schools, what has been the subject of this whole book, that is, namely the horrible discipline problems that we were faced with. In an attempt to address this crucial issue, Mayor O'Looney proposed hiring retired police officers at the very reasonable fee of $150 per day to patrol our troubled schools' hallways and to start to make a dent in the chaos and bedlam plaguing the worst of the failing schools. Unfortunately the teachers' union would have none of this! Instead they insisted that teachers' union "Disciplinary Administrators" be put on the job and paid top union scale ($85,000) per year. To start off with, they suggested that six of these administrators be hired, but as our town fathers couldn't come up with the extra half a million in our educational budget, nothing was done. Since the Mayor's suggestion was shot down, and didn't go through either, the schools continue to languish in the deplorable state that I've described! By the way, to get the extra two school days, the city fathers had to give the teachers a six percent pay raise, albeit over a two- year period.

Speaking about teachers' unions, although individually I liked (and often felt sorry for) the teachers who were my co-workers, I tend to agree with John Stossel in his contention that they are one of the main reasons why public schools today are as messed up as I have been telling you about. He writes: "Education reformers have a name for the resistance (to educational reform): the education 'Blob' which includes the teachers unions, but also janitors and principals unions, school boards, PTA bureaucrats, local politicians and so on. They hold power because the government's monopoly on K-12 education eliminates most competition. Kids are assigned to schools, and a bureaucrat decides who goes where and who learns what. Over time, its tentacles expand and strangle attempts to reform. Since they have no fear of losing their jobs to competitors, monopoly bureaucrats can resist innovation for decades. In New York City, unionized teachers protesting outside my office said: 'Our rules are good and necessary, and if cities would let us train teachers and run schools, we'd do a great job....We have the expertise, intelligence, the experience to do what works for children'

They said if charter schools must exist, the union should run one, and they 'would create a school where all parents would want to send their children.' So

New York City gave the United Federation of Teachers a charter school of its own. The union boss called it an 'oasis.'

But what happened? Today the teachers' union school is one of New York's worst. It got a 'D' on its city report card. Only a third of its students read at grade level. And the school still lost a million dollars. I assume the union staffed the school with some of the best teachers. The union knew we were watching. But with union rules, and the Blob's bureaucracy, they failed miserably.

I really want to ask union leaders why they hate competition, but they won't come on my Fox television show."

You give it to 'em John! And what about the fiasco that's going through now? All over the country liberal politicians are raising the mandatory age for school attendance up to seventeen! Many states have already enacted this (my very deep blue state included) and suffering inner city school districts are buckling under the burden. What does this accomplish? We just have bigger and bigger lummoxes, who wanted to drop out of school years ago, pined down into a hated environment where they don't want to be! And, pray tell, what do you think these chained-up monsters are going to do during their last year of enforced servitude? I tell you what- they're going to be making one hell of a racket and a commotion and be disrupting every classroom to the max- so that YOUR CHILD SITTING NEXT TO THEM can't hear himself think and learns next to nothing! Of course, if a kid is a little behind and WANTS to stay in school beyond the age of sixteen, to me that's a different matter. The liberal politicians pushing these types of changes tell us that they're doing it because they "love education." Personally, I think they're doing it because they love the booty plowing into their campaign war chests from the teachers' unions. We have enough problems in this country without turning our schools into prisons for wayward teenagers and into employment factories for twenty-something suburban kids who are graduating college without any desire to go into science, business or industry! Phooey!

To show you just how wacko some of these teachers' unions can be, the "Investors Business Daily" in Dec. of 2012 reported that the California Federation of Teachers' website featured a cartoon narrated by Ed Asner. At the end of the cartoon there was a fat cartoon character identified as "the rich" urinating on the poor! Outrageous as this may sound I must admit that I wasn't completely surprised.

James W. Shine

    Once again, I can't stress enough how much I liked and respected the young teachers who I worked with at Williams but, nevertheless, as time went on I slowly began to realize that I was dealing with people who had never come out of their cocoon. When they were younger they had been students in school, then they went to college and were students there, now they were back in school again teaching students in a school. Get the connection? All their short lives, all they've ever known, is school, school, school! Few of them had any experience in the real world of free enterprise, business, or manufacturing. True, some had worked part-time going through college as waitresses, lifeguards, clerks, etc., but in my mind that hardly counts. When I told them that I had had a career in business and finance before I had walked into Williams, they kind of looked at me askance. I could hear a little whispering, and I kind of caught the 'vibe off them like "What in heck is he doing here?" Their perception (erroneous as it may be) was that everybody in the private sector was making "big bucks" and that they were just "poor teachers." Yes, as I pointed out earlier, many of them were carrying hefty student loan balances, and raising young families, and in my State which is one of the most expensive in the nation when it comes to living expenses, this can be a struggle, but they were nowhere near as poorly paid as they thought they were! They mostly agreed with the guy who to many of them was a hero (Pres. Obama) that the "rich", whom I think that they identified as anybody above middle management in the private sector, should be paying their "fair share." That way, they thought, maybe our crumbling schools could be fixed. They never seemed to realize that ninety percent of our district's funding went to fund their salaries! Like most twenty somethings coming out of college now a days many of them had a socialist, or at least a "big government can do anything" bent.

    As a matter of fact, we even had a quasi-Communist at Williams! Remember Mr. Peru, the school librarian that I had mentioned earlier? In addition to being a fine teacher and a great helper for Mr. Rodrigo with the in-house suspension kids, he unfortunately espoused some very controversial ideas. This Puerto Rican gentleman had made quite a few pilgrimages to Cuba, greatly admired Fidel Castro, and thought of Cuba as a workers paradise! He was constantly railing on about "Yankee imperialism" and claiming that our "American Empire" was an evil entity causing most of the suffering in the world today. Unfortunately he didn't just keep these anti-American ideas to himself, but rather foisted them on the students in a pretty aggressive manner. I don't know where he found them, but he located books that depicted our country's history in a rather unflattering light, and then assigned them for the students to read while afterwards conducting classroom discussions. I vividly remember one book that described our Westward-Hoing cowboy pioneers as genocidal maniacs who enjoyed killing and torturing the Indians. Oops! I forgot, we call them "native Americans" now. (Please remember that I'm in my sixties) The story went on to tell about a particularly brutal cowboy bounty hunter who was paid cash on the barrelhead for each and every Native American scalp he took. In the book this bloody handed murderer, who had killed the boy's parents, was ruthlessly chasing this poor, non- violent Native American boy (coincidentally the exact same age as Mr. Peru's students) helter-skelter throughout the West! I don't know what this dedicated teacher was trying to do. But if he was trying to instill some sort of "white guilt" into his audience he was definitely preaching to the wrong choir. Eighty percent of the kids in his classroom were black or Hispanic! I know reader that you might fear that this sort of inflammatory stuff might cause the black and Hispanic students to become angry, and turn violently on the true minority at Williams (the white kids), but luckily for us all that didn't happen. As I mentioned before, the young people today see themselves as living in a post-racial world and they see all of this drama as irrelevant ancient history. No lurid melodramas of evil gringos of a hundred and fifty years ago were enough to re-kindle race hatreds in these children. Those hatreds, I'm sure, died a long time ago, back in their parents'- if not grandparents'- time. Still, I wonder what Mr. Peru's motives were. I'm also shocked to realize how drastically society's attitudes towards everything have changed. Heck, when I was a kid, the cowboys were the good guys (I always wanted to be one) and the Indians (oops, Native Americans) were the heartless villains who went around scalping everybody! In addition dear reader, a story like this must give you a certain amount of pause, and even alarm. Do you know what sort of values are being instilled in your children at their school? Are YOUR values being taught, or are your kids being force-fed the anti-American values of someone like Mr. Peru (name changed)? You should find out!

    Mr. Peru described the children of the ghetto, who populated our schools, as "throw away" children. He blamed this phenomenon as being the inevitable result of a heartless America whose strings were secretly being pulled by greedy Anglo businessmen out in the suburbs, who he said "didn't give a rat's ass" about the unfortunate brown kids who had the bad luck to have been born into our cities. When I see what Barrack Obama and so many others have accomplished, I disagree with him completely, and have my doubts that these students functioned at the low level that they did simply as a result of persistent societal racism. Still, he was far from alone in his thinking, as his ideas were quite widespread throughout the teaching cadre, many of whom did not really expect very much from these kids, as they had come from such a downtrodden background. Kind of what President Obama was talking about when he mentioned the "bigotry of low expectations."

In stark opposition to the gloomy musings of these educators who posited that the black and Hispanic youth of the inner cities inevitably had to fail due to the lingering effects of white discrimination, much more positive voices were raised as well. In 2012 when Mayor O'Looney was elected in our city, he brought into power with him a young African-American man, who was in a unique position to do something about the ills that were dragging us down.

Greg Hadley, for nearly a decade, had run a community learning center in our most blighted and rundown North End neighborhood. This educational and social center where kids from chaotic home environments could safely do their homework, was right at the epicenter of the worst crime and violence in the city.

When this non-profit center lost its funding a couple of years ago due to budget cuts, Greg Hadley continued working there for free. So I think that maybe we ought to listen to someone like him! Diametrically in contrast to what our city's previous black "leaders" for the past few decades had been saying (you know the race hustlers who put all the blame on "whitey"), Alderman Hadley said at his swearing in ceremony, "I am challenging the African-American community to work better to come up with some strategies and plans to help our city and our nation. This is the time. We can no longer sit back and wait for things to happen. You're either part of the solution, or you're part of the problem." Bravo!

But bright hopes for the future aside, our teachers' attitudes weren't quite as sanguine. During the past year, we've come to look upon teaching as an occupation, like policemen or firefighters, whose members are often heroes. In Newtown, Connecticut (quite close to me) and in Moore, Oklahoma (far away) teachers put their lives on the line for their students. Some even lost their lives!

I want nothing that I've written in this book to cause any of you, dear readers, to lessen the esteem that you hold our country's teachers in by even the smallest, tiniest iota. Our teachers are brave and heroic. But they're NOT STUPID! When I asked the teachers I was working for at Williams if they would want THEIR OWN CHILDREN to attend our school, they answered with a unanimous "No!" They thought that we had an OK school- FOR SOMEBODY ELSE'S KIDS. In this, these twenty-something and thirty something young adults again mirrored the sentiments of their hero- Barrack Obama. President Obama has always been a staunch supporter of our Nation's public schools, yet when he was elected President and moved to Washington, he made sure that his own daughters were never enrolled in that district's minority majority public school system! A typical "limousine liberal", he loves to tell you what you should do with your kids, but as far as his own kids go, that's a different kettle of fish. These people don't practice what they preach, and we should look more closely at what they do rather than what they say.

Educational reform is by its very nature a slow process, and there's no doubt that my city has begun the journey down that long road and is doing some very positive things, but nevertheless, because of the intrinsic inertia of the "educational blob" that John Stossel talked about, you'll probably have to zoom ahead to when your children's children are strapping on their first bookbags before all of our inner city schools are working as they should. I'm afraid that that dour prediction applies to my city's schools as well!

14
What My State and Our Nation are Doing

Due to exclusionary zoning my tiny state is said to be the most segregated one in the nation. In 149 out of 169 of our towns each house must sit on an acre or two of land. These picturesque, tony, New England towns generally have few apartments, or any other sort of low-income housing within their borders and anyone at all who has any pretensions to belonging to the middle class has moved out there. At the polar opposite of this spectrum, four out of five our largest cities have square miles upon square miles of low-income and section 8 housing and, in addition, these cities (including mine) are precisely where our State government has seen fit to place over 90% of our soup kitchens, homeless shelters, halfway houses, food stamp and welfare offices. By the way, our State's welfare payments and food stamp allotments are among the highest in the country, and our Section 8 housing program is the most liberal in the nation! To further insure, for God only knows what reason, that tens of thousands more low income people (and illegal aliens) pour into these designated cities our political leaders (almost all of whom live in the suburbs) have created a program called "sanctuary cities." In "sanctuary cities" illegal aliens can live normal American lives without having to look over their shoulders or worry about their immigration status. The INS isn't welcome in a sanctuary city! To further entice illegal aliens to move here, our "leaders' just this year even put through a new law enabling them to get official State drivers licenses, and drive about on our streets regardless of whether they're citizens or not. This frightening dichotomy between the rich and poor has caused my State to be placed fourth from last in economic competitiveness according to the American Legislative Exchange Council. Generations of "white flight" have completed the process of turning these once vibrant industrial cities into the vast repositories of the permanent welfare and food stamp dependent underclass that they now are. These, by and large, were the parents of my students!

For years (despite lawsuits by inner city parents trying to change things) this educational achievement gap that was the inevitable result of this "rich state/poor state" divide could be swept under the rug by the powers that be, but in recent years the batteries of standardized tests given to all our state's kids mandated by the federal government, have brought this gap into our consciousness in a way that nobody can ignore. And again, it isn't just because that our inner city schools ARE SO BAD that we have a problem. What widens the gap is that our suburban schools ARE SO GOOD! For example, less than ten miles from Williams was a public school district that was accredited to be one of the best in the nation. Our state was full of these types of outrageous contrasts!

In 2010 a new governor was elected in our deepest of the deep blue states. This jovial gentleman had, for ten years, been the mayor of one of our five largest cities so he was very well aware of our state's worst in the nation educational achievement gap. His take on this issue was simple. He blamed the teachers! I'm not sure I agree with him on this. I made the analogy before that we wouldn't want to pull a dentist's license just because his young charges don't floss between office visits; yet Governor Maloney seemed perfectly willing to pull teacher's licenses if their students continue to do poorly on the State's standardized tests. Where's the fairness in that! Still, I think he did bring up some valid points.

The governor wanted to do something about teacher tenure. In our state, up until now, once a teacher has served for three years, they pretty much are untouchable. You may remember the stories published a few years back in the "New York Daily News" how in New York City, at any given time, up to seven hundred teachers were being paid full salaries NOT TO TEACH! Instead, these teachers were being paid to report to what were called "rubber rooms", where they sat around and read novels or played cards while meanwhile collecting their full salaries. They did this for an average period of nineteen months, while the city jumped through the hoops required by the union contacts and the law in order to get rid of them. So, once you've got yourself established as a certified teacher, you pretty much have job security unless you're a pedophile or shoot a student! As teacher's evaluations are generally done by the various school principals, who by and large were the teacher's friends, most evaluations come out as being "good" or "excellent", and obtaining tenure is a piece of cake. The evaluation process is highly subjective and, unless there's some sort of major teacher/principal conflict, it's all pretty much of a rubber stamp anyways. Unlike doctors or lawyers, national studies have shown that only a few hundred teachers every year, out of hundreds of thousands, are ever removed for incompetence or serious malfeasance.

At Williams too, I saw the horrible effects that having substandard teachers can have. Remember Chapter Four (The Not So Good Teachers)? Another thing that I noticed was that teacher's abilities (or lack of same) to successfully function in their classroom fluctuated dramatically from year to year! I'll give you a couple of examples. I mentioned, in a quite negative way back in that chapter, a teacher I called "Mrs. McGinty." She was an older woman who had just gone into teaching as a second career, and I had made much of her woefully inadequate classroom management skills. Well, back when I was writing that it was both my own and Mrs. McGinty's first year of service at Williams. Three years later, as I was finishing my stint, she had blossomed into a quite serviceable teacher and her management skills were MORE than adequate. I almost regretted what I had written about her earlier in this book- although what I wrote was true at the time!

On the other hand, it went the opposite way as well. Another teacher, who I'll let remain nameless, lost her "Mo-JO" while I was there. Although she had been a perfectly adequate teacher back in 2009, by the time I left three years later, she had deteriorated into a cartoon caricature of herself screaming at the kids all the time and being listened to by none of them. What caused this? I'm not sure. Maybe the kids changed in the intervening years, and certainly this teacher aged (she reached her mid-60's), her mother developed dementia and she became preoccupied with out-of-school responsibilities; but I'm afraid one of the biggest reasons was that she didn't keep up with newest technologies and the teenagers really began to look down on her. When you look at examples like this you begin to think that teacher tenure is kind of a sketchy concept to start with and that maybe, Governor Maloney is right when he wants to reform it and, more importantly, to bring in objective, meaningful yearly teacher evaluations.

Of course, the educational blob fought him tooth and nail on this!

Eventually, after much wrangling, a much-watered down version of the governor's proposal was passed into law. In the final draft, student's test scores on the state's standardized tests were allowed to count for between 35-40% of the teacher's evaluation. Input from the teacher's fellow staff members and the principal would still constitute approximately 60% of their score (heck, we can't completely dismantle the "old boy network") and a small input was to be factored in from the students themselves and their parents. But then, lo and behold, when the educational establishment began to incorporate these reforms into the existing educational department's rule and regulations, it was determined that implementing them was going to cost millions and millions of dollars!

It was determined that the school principals alone would be unable to perform these much more complex state mandated teacher evaluations. First of all, they were simply too busy, everyone knows that principals spent 95% of their time on student disciplinary issues (I can attest to that!) and, besides; many principals lacked the computer savvy needed to factor in the data from the kids' testing into the teacher's competency results. So, it was decided that each district would have to hire testing and evaluation professionals and IT people to help the principals. As with many other educational reform measures that we've been discussing, money in the districts was tight, so the new teacher evaluation model is being postponed into future years! My hunch is that Governor Maloney's teacher tenure and evaluation idea, modest proposal though it is, is going to be helpful for our schools, but it will probably be quite a few years before it is fully implemented and we have enough data to decide. Meanwhile our failing inner city schools will have to struggle along with the significant numbers of burned-out teachers and complete incompetents that we've been burdened with up until now.

My state is also sticking its toe into the concept of charter schools. Charter schools are an idea WHOSE TIME HAS COME! Charter schools are private, usually for profit, institutions where children are educated using proven, workable methods that may, or may not, have the blessings of the educational blob. Among the tools employed by these schools are longer school hours, more days in the school year, smaller class sizes, and a "no excuses" attitude whereby recalcitrant, disruptive students are just kicked out and that's it! Only one tenth of all charter schools are unionized so that, unlike our public schools, they're not run by the teachers' unions. Throughout the US there are about six thousand charter schools, which is only about six percent of the total number of public schools. In my state, the numbers are even worse, only two percent of our schools are charters, which is why I say that we're only "dipping our toe." Charter schools function in much the same way that parochial and other religious schools did. These institutions were quite common in our cities thirty or forty years ago, but have become rather scarce as America has become more secular. That's too bad, as they provided a wonderful education, back in their time, for millions of students (including yours truly).

The educational blob and the teachers' unions fight the idea of charter schools tooth and nail. They claim that sending our children to charter schools will bring back the era of school segregation. But that's not necessarily so! John Stossel writes:

"The Blob claims public education is 'the great equalizer.' Rich and poor and different races mix and learn together. It's a beautiful concept. But it is a lie. Rich parents buy homes in neighborhoods with better schools.

As a result, public- I mean GOVERNMENT- schools are more racially segregated than private schools. One survey found public schools were significantly more likely to be almost entirely white or entirely minority. Another found that at private schools, students of different races were more likely to sit together.

The Blob's most powerful argument is that poor people need government-run schools. How could poor people possibly afford tuition?

Well, consider some truly destitute places. James Tooley spends most of his time in the poorest parts of Africa, India and China. Those countries copied America's 'free public education,' and Tooley wanted to see how that's worked out. What he learned is that in India and China, where Kids outperform American kids on tests, it's not because they attended the government's free schools. Government schools are horrible. So even in the worst slums, parents try to send their kids to private, for-profit schools.

How can the world's poorest people afford tuition? And why would they pay for what their governments offer for free?

Tooley says parents with meager resources still sacrifice to send their kids to private schools because the private owner does something that's virtually impossible in public schools: replace teachers who do not teach. Government teachers in India and Africa have jobs for life, just like American teachers. Many sleep on the job. Some don't even show up for work.

As a result, says Tooley, 'the majority of (poor) schoolchildren are in private school.' Even small villages have as many as six private schools, 'and these schools outperform government schools at a fraction of the teacher cost.'

As in America, government officials scoff at private schools and the parents who choose them. A woman who runs government schools in Nigeria calls such parents 'ignoramuses.' They aren't – and thanks to competition, their children won't be either.

Low-income Americans are far richer than the poor people of China, India and Africa. So if competitive private education can work in Beijing, Calcutta and Nairobi, it can work in the United States. We just need to get around the Blob."

Yup, as usual our good friend John is right on the money here. But forget about far away foreign countries, what do statistics here in America show? Well, according to joint studies done by the Boston Foundation and MIT's School Effectiveness and Inequality Initiative, not only do charter schools do especially well in urban areas but results show that, percentage-wise, TWICE the number of charter school students are accepted for ADVANCED PLACEMENT as well as being TWICE AS LIKELY to be granted STATE FINANCIAL COLLEGE SCHOLARSHIPS! Ray Fisman, a professor at Columbia Business School wrote, "In their short history, charter schools have shown enormous promise in improving the education of many disadvantaged students. We shouldn't lose sight of that, and we should be open to the innovations coming out of charters that might be applied to a broader set of schools."

Even in my post-industrial city, which I often jokingly referred to as "the Jewel of New England" small private schools are doing wonders! Right down the street from Williams, a for-profit group who called themselves "The Children's Community School," was receiving plaudits and accolades from every expert and authority that has come to visit them. Operating out of an old, abandoned Catholic school building these good people are running an elementary school taking in children with the exact same demographics, and from the exact same geographic area, that my own kids had come from (in other words "the hood"). But instead of the chaos I had witnessed, when they worked with these students politeness and respect for staff were the watchwords and test scores were in the highest percentiles. The tuition they charged? Three hundred and fifty dollars per year! This is as opposed to the $18,000+ per year that my city is spending on a per pupil basis for public education. The latest news flash is that the Community School people are now applying to become a state sponsored charter school whereby they would get city/state vouchers and could greatly expand the numbers of kids that they would be able to take in and help. My only hope is that my city and my state will get their act together and MAKE THIS HAPPEN!

As a matter of fact when they see what charter schools can accomplish, some of the educational Blob's educrats are starting to drop their long held opposition. For example in my state's capital city, one of the state's lowest performing educational districts, they have in recent years spent millions of dollars on out-of-town charter schools where they've been busing the inner-city children. Now, in exchange, district officials get to use the higher scores from the charter school kids to boost the district's over-all scores when they report back to the state and federal government! "We're basically buying their test scores". said Robert Cotto Jr., a member of that city's school board. "Our scores have gone up through the roof," he gushed.

While it's unclear just how much this kind of sneaky technique has boosted my capital city's scores, it must be a lot, as a bill pending in the State Legislature would allow nine other low-performing school districts to start doing the same! Well, even if they're good for nothing else, at least it looks like charter schools are a big help at getting the federal educrats off of the state and local educrats' butts! I don't mean to sound cynical, but that's OK with me, AT LEAST IT HELPS THE KIDS!

Again, trying to do something about the failing schools (ninety percent of which are in our big cities with their massive welfare populations), the state designated failing educational districts as "Alliance Districts" and the worst schools within those districts as "turn-around" schools. For each turn-around school a "turn around committee" was established. Millions of dollars were earmarked for our low-performing city district and, in particular, for some of our most dysfunctional schools, and you would have thought that locally everyone would have been ecstatic. YOU WOULD HAVE BEEN WRONG! As Robert Kennedy said, "Progress is a nice word. But change is its motivator. And change has its enemies." It sure does! One of William's feeder elementary schools (I mentioned it before as being the school in the national news whose principal wouldn't let the students celebrate XMAS) was down in the record books as having the sixth lowest student testing scores in the whole state. Yet, when the state's educational experts came in and removed that controversial principal who was known for his easy going ways, and not backing up the teachers when they tried to discipline the students, the whole community erupted in protest! All that we heard about in the news was how racist it all was, and that the one and only black principal in our city was getting the boot because of discrimination.

In sympathy with the parents in the neighborhood, I must say that the principal who was replaced was a glad-handing people skills type person who was very well liked, and that the experts who came in to take over were rather ham-handed in their methods. For example, these educrats immediately stopped the parents from attending the morning pep rallies at the school that the old principal had initiated. Locking the parents out of the school didn't go over well! Eventually, for better or worse, the educrats decided to discontinue the pep rallies altogether. Then too, I'm not too sure how well these $5,000 a week experts in their three- piece suits would go over anyways as they pontificated in a hundred year old school smack in area replete with crack houses and most known for drive-by shootings! Still, the proof is in the pudding, and the scores of their children alone should have been enough of a factor for the parents to accept the need for change, instead of seeing everything around them as a racist soap opera! Who knows? Someday, for the kids' sake; maybe the experts from on high in their three-piece suits, and the parents from the 'hood', will be able to sit down and have a nice discussion as to how exactly schools like this should be run. But if might not be anytime soon!

In 2013 my state, as well as most of the others throughout America, adopted a new, more stringent school curriculum being pushed forward by the federal government called "common core standards." These standards raised the bar and mandated an enhanced learning level academically for every grade level. Many well-meaning conservatives questioned this development as they felt that it was an unwarranted intrusion of federal power into the local educational process. They also feared that all of the government data-gathering on the students that is part and parcel of this program is just another step down the road to a "big brother" state that is every day becoming more of a reality. The constant scandals that we read about daily about the government spying on our own people (the IRS, the NSA etc.) certainly go along way to validating these fears! Still, when I look at the lamentable state of our public educational system today, and the profound ignorance displayed by so many of its students, I can see no other alternative rather than to try and raise our standards!

James W. Shine

An interesting aspect of the common core educational model is that there are shifts in the METHODS of teaching as well as just an elevation of the learning curve. In contrast to current teaching modalities with their emphasis on rote memorization (not that our inner city schools are doing a great job on that one either), the common core inspired teacher is being encouraged to turn her classroom into a discussion area. It's suggested that instead of standing in front of the class, the teacher might want to place the desks in a horseshoe shape and kind of function as a discussion moderator. GOOD LUCK WITH THAT ONE!!

Unless you have teachers like Ms. Stango or Ms. Brenner in each and every classroom, there's no way that something like that is going to work in any type of inner city school that I'm familiar with. As I mentioned before, discussions were exactly the kind of thing that we couldn't do. All the children would scream and talk at once, would never stop and listen to each other, and seemed oblivious to the "one person speaks at a time" rule. It was a veritable Tower of Babel each and every day! Trying to shut them up I would say to the kids, "God gave you two ears and only one mouth, so he meant for you to listen twice as much as you talk. Besides, when you open your mouth, whatever comes out of it, you already know. On the other hand, when you listen there is the possibility that you might actually LEARN something new!" Usually when I said this, they'd be stunned and would be quite for a few seconds, but then the wise guys would start hooting and scoffing at me, so the familiar chaos would return. One time though, Andre a recent Jamaican immigrant boy blurted out, "Every day we learn something new from Mr. Shine!" That made me feel good.

Often times there's something funny about educational reform proposals; not as in "funny"- Ha! Ha!; but as in "funny" peculiar. Ronald Reagan said, "If you serve a child a rotten hamburger in America, federal, state and local agencies will investigate you, summon you, close you down, whatever. But if you provide a child with a rotten education, nothing happens, except that you're liable to be given more money to do it with." Yep, give them more money (and hire more teachers), seems to be the thrust behind the majority of educational reform proposals floating around today! Just as the big national push to mandate school attendance up until age seventeen is going to be an enormously expensive proposition (and teachers' employment program), so the push on the other end, to mandate Pre-K education for every child, will have the exact same result. Universal Pre-K is one of President Obama's favorite proposals when it comes to fixing America's schools despite the scanty evidence that it would do any good at all. He proposes it despite the fact that his own Department of Health and Human Services, while evaluating the Head Start Pre-K program in 2011 found that, "advantages children gained during their Head Start and aged four years yielded only a few statistically significant differences in outcomes at the end of 1st grade for the sample as a whole." The study went on to say, "The benefits of access to Head Start at age four are largely absent by 1st grade for the program population as a whole." Now I'm not saying that Pre-K and Head Start haven't helped countless kids get ready for school when they've been lagging behind their peers, but this is something that each and every parent should be evaluating for their child on an individualized basis. PEOPLE ARE INDIVIDUALS SO YOU CAN'T GENERALIZE. And, of course, children are people so sweeping mandates effecting ALL CHILDREN and ALL PARENTS are something that ought to be avoided. Just anecdotally, I'll tell you this, amidst all the tumult and chaos at Williams I'd often ask for a show of hands as to which kids in each classroom had attended Pre-school or Head Start. The majority of hands would go up and, for the life of me; I couldn't detect any differences in the performance or behavior of the students who had that early educational exposure as opposed to those who hadn't. I'm therefore not really surprised by the results found by DHHS in their study!

A word or two about President Obama. I've mentioned that the Williams' kids loved him, and that he was a tremendously important role model for them as well as for the millions of other minority children throughout America. But despite that, he didn't get to the pinnacle of success in this country based on the strength of his ideas alone. Rather his meteoric rise, in my humble opinion, was due to three entirely different factors. First, he benefited from the votes of millions of minority (soon to be majority) voters who wanted to vote for "one of us," second, countless white voters gave him their vote due to white guilt- with the thinking that they could prove to themselves they weren't racists by voting for a black man; and, finally, he is (as I can personally attest) an absolutely first-rate, spell binding orator. Nevertheless, and despite the fact that I think his proposal for universal pre-school is a non-starter, President Obama did a world of good for all of our inner city students with his Morehouse College commencement address this year.

Now I know that Bill Cosby (and others) have been saying what the President has said for years, but with the credibility that the he enjoys, it's my fondest hope that now this message will start to sink in!

Morehouse College is a small all black, all male historic Georgian institution of higher learning. Of course, it boggles the mind to think what the politically correct types would do with someone who started an all white, all male college now-a-days, they'd probably recommend that their severed head be placed on a spike, well let's forget about that; there certainly couldn't have been a better venue for President Obama to give this important address. In the commencement the President discussed the twin pathologies that have been turning our inner cities into violence-prone war zones and making our permanent welfare under-class (and their children) so resistant to education and self- improvement. These pathologies are the pathology of fatherlessness and the "I am a helpless victim" attitude that so permeates our ghetto dwellers and is passed on to their children.

Across the nation, more than one-fourth of all children live in single-parent homes. The vast majority of these children live with their mothers. When children don't have stable relationships with their dads, marked by frequent involvement, they are more susceptible to depression and are more likely to abuse drugs, or demonstrate delinquent behavior.

According to census department statistics, children who live in single-parent households are 82% more likely to experience child poverty. With the unmarried birth rate high among young women with the lowest levels of education, single-mother households now comprise more than half of all families living in poverty. Without the relative financial stability marriage can provide, single parents and their children are at a greater risk of government dependence. Of the $1 trillion spent on welfare funding to low-income families with children, almost three-quarters went to single parent, overwhelmingly fatherless, homes!

When fathers play an active role in the lives of their children, they make a tangible difference. Children whose fathers spent time with them doing day-to-day activities such as homework, eating dinner or playing sports earned better grades than their peers who had less access to fathers. It is vital for a father to play an active role in the lives of his children, particularly by being married to the mother of his kids!

Truin Huntle, executive director of First Things First of Greater Richmond, Virginia (where sixty percent of children are reported to be living in fatherless households) said; "We see more people beginning to give some credence to the idea that fathers are crucial because they are looking for the root cause of other issues like childhood poverty and poor performance in school. Father absenteeism, broken homes, broken marriages and teen pregnancy are continually being found as the root cause of these problems."

If I am sure of anything in this world, it is that families (or what's left of them) are the first and most important molders of whatever values the young child is going to start school with. Noted sociologist Friedrich Heyek agrees with us on this, he wrote in his work "The Constitution of Liberty" that, "Families are the primary transmitters of human capital-habits, mores, education. Hence families, much more than other social institutions or programs, are the determiners of academic and vocational success."

As far as the "I am a victim of racism" syndrome goes, I can verify that one personally. There wasn't a month that went by at Williams, that out of the clear blue, some black child would call me a racist for no other reason than that I was old, fat and white (and, oh yeah, I asked them to do a little work)! These were young teens and pre-teens, where did they get that idea? From their paranoid parents? Possibly. But we do foster a lot of white guilt in this country, and race hustlers pick up on it, and use it to keep themselves in business, and to keep the old perpetual victim philosophy in the 'hood' alive.

I'll give you just one example. In Wisconsin, that state's Department of Public Instruction works with the Volunteers in Service to America (VISTA) to go around in public schools to "educate" white students about their intrinsic amount of racism. These "Volunteers" (who by the way are paid) are conducting what they call "consciousness raising." White students are urged to wear white wristbands "as a reminder of your privilege." It's also suggested that they "put a note on your computer screen to remind you to think about your privilege in being a white person." White kids are asked to conduct an internal dialogue with themselves and to ask themselves; "What are the ways that the privilege of being a white kid worked out for me today?' and "What can I do today to eliminate my special white-person privileges?" Wow!

President Obama launched a head-on attack on these pernicious trends that have hobbled generations of inner city kids in his Morehouse speech. He said: "In troubled neighborhoods all across this country-many of them heavily African-American-too few of our citizens have role models to guide them…. We know that too many young men in our community continue to make bad choices. And I have to say, growing up, I made quite a few myself. Sometimes I wrote off my failings as just another example of the world trying to keep a black man down. I had a tendency sometimes to make excuses for me not doing the right thing. But one of the things that you have learned here is that there's no longer any room for excuses. I understand that there's a common fraternity creed here at Morehouse: 'Excuses are tools of the incompetent to build bridges to nowhere and monuments of nothingness.' Well, we've got no time for excuses….In today's hyperconnected, hypercompetitive world, with millions of young people from China, India and Brazil- many of whom started out with a whole lot less than all of you did-all of them entering the global workforce alongside you, nobody is going to give you anything that you have not earned.

Nobody cares how tough your upbringing was. Nobody cares if you suffered some discrimination. And moreover, you have to remember that whatever you've gone through, it pales in comparison to the hardships that previous generations endured-and they overcame them. AND IF THEY OVERCAME THEM, YOU CAN OVERCOME THEM, TOO (Emphasis mine)."

Regarding the importance of being a good father he continued: "Keep setting an example for what it means to be a man. Be the best husband to your wife, or your boyfriend, or your partner. Be the best father you can be to your children. Because nothing is more important.

I was raised by a heroic single mom, wonderful grandparents- made incredible sacrifices for me. And I know that there are moms and grandparents here today who did the same thing for all of you. But I sure wish I had had a father who was not only a parent, but involved. Didn't know my Dad. And so my whole life, I've tried to be for Michelle and my girls what my father was not for my mother and me. I WANT TO BREAK THAT CYCLE WHERE A FATHER IS NOT AT HOME (my emphasis)-where a father is not helping to raise that son or daughter. I want to be a better father, a better husband, a better man.

I know that when I am on my deathbed someday, I will not be thinking about any particular legislation I passed, I will not be thinking about a policy I promoted; I will not be thinking about the speech I gave, I will not be thinking about the Nobel Prize I received. I will be thinking about that walk that I took with my daughters. I'll be thinking about a lazy afternoon with my wife. I'll be thinking about sitting around the dinner table and seeing them happy and healthy and knowing that they were loved. And I'll be thinking about whether I did right by all of them."

If you look backward a few pages in this text I'm sure you can see, dear reader, that I'm no star-struck fan of President Obama's. Yet; there can be no doubt that if the children in our inner cities today (and their parents) took his message at Morehouse to heart, internalized it, and began to put it into practice, that it would do MORE GOOD than if we spend trillions of dollars on educational reform! Besides, America, this is one problem that we just can't spend our way out of. Even if we throw trillions in that direction (which knowing our history we're probably going to do), if past practice is any guide, most of it is going to be frittered away by the educrats and their incompetent bureaucracy anyways!

Finally, when I talk about what my state and the nation are doing, I have to mention that my state's governor, Governor Malloy (oops, I used his real name), was a dedicated follower of President Obama's. A firm believer, as is the President in early childhood education, he established a new state department to further that goal with joint state and federal funding of 359 million dollars for start up costs. He also wanted to fund an expansion of our state's charter schools, which would have been a great idea, as we haven't opened a new one since 2007.

But suddenly, SUDDENLY, my State became very short of money for educational reform, priorities shifted, SCHOOL SECURITY became the paramount issue, and 34 million had to be spent on doors and locks!

In December of 2012, while I was writing this book, a deranged young maniac who was reportedly obsessed by violent video games (like many of my students), burst into an elementary school in Newtown, a leafy suburb only twenty miles from my down-trodden inner city, and brutally shot and massacred twenty innocent, little first graders. He also shot and killed six educators there, including two teacher's aides (basically paras), Rachel D'avino and Anne Marie Murphy. Unless you've been living under a bridge for the last year, I'm sure you can now guess what State I'm writing from! The perpetrator, Adam Lanza, was only twenty years old, and if ever we've had a wake-up call as to what a lousy job that we're doing in this country when it comes to inculcating decent values into the minds of our young people, this incident should be it. MAY THE ANGELS BRING THE SOULS OF THESE SLAUGTERED INNOCENTS, AND THEIR TEACHER-PROTECTORS, TO HEAVEN. And, MAY THEY REST IN PEACE.

♥♥♥♥♥♥♥♥♥♥♥♥♥♥♥♥♥♥♥♥♥♥♥♥♥

15

What More Can Be Done

Despite everything our nation is doing (and all the money we're spending) our performance in the educational field is as lousy as a hundred year old man's at a swinger's convention! Although we spend, on a per pupil basis, 50% more than the average developed country, we rank in the bottom third in global student performance in science and math behind, China, Singapore, South Korea, and Finland. Actually, we spend more per pupil for education than ANY OTHER COUNTRY ON EARTH except for Switzerland (where social problems are nearly non-existent), yet seventeen other countries graduate more scientists than we do! Like I said, this doesn't look like a problem that we can simply spend our way out of. So what tangible, nuts and bolts things, can we do to improve our miserable results? WE CAN:

- Totally remake our child's failing school like the character Jaime Fitzpatrick did in the 2012 movie "Won't back down." In that film Jaime (the main character), who was living in the inner city and whose daughter Mollyia was going to a horrible school, became disappointed and enraged when Mollyia's name wasn't picked in the lottery for one of the few spots in a good school down the street. These high-stakes lotteries for the scarce spots at good schools, such a source of hope and trepidation for inner city parents, are also featured in the 2011 educational reform movie "Waiting for Superman." I highly recommend, dear reader, that you go and see both of these films! Anyways, when the dyslexic Mollyia's number didn't come up for the good school, her mother felt that she had no choice but to take the bull by the horns and launch an all-out crusade to change the way things were done at

Mollyia's current school. Possibly speaking for all conscientious frustrated inner city parents Jaime says, " This school is failing but I can't afford to move so I'm screwed." Doing a little research, this mother finds out -as did this author- that 25% of American children are functionally illiterate when they're finished with school (remember that in the dropout factories that we and this movie are speaking about half of the kids never even graduate) so she definitely wasn't going to buy the educrats advice that she should "wait." Another character in the film, Nona Alberts a good teacher at Mollyia's school who decides to help Jaime, says "Waiting means doing nothing." When asleep at the switch fellow teachers try to dissuade Nona from helping change things by blaming the problems at their school on the blighted neighborhood the school is in, she shoots back "Change the school and you'll change the neighborhood!" Jaime warns the establishment opposing her, "You know those mothers you hear about who pick up two ton trucks off of their children? I'm one of those mothers!" It's all very dramatic. As you can probably guess (surprise! surprise!) the teacher's union fought our intrepid reformers every step of the way. Albert Shanker's, past president of the American Federation of Teachers old quote is brought up, "When school children start to pay union dues I'll start representing the children instead of the teachers." But in the end, as always happens in Hollywood, good triumphs and a great victory occurs when a majority of the parents and teachers at the school are won over, they go to the school board, and our reformers are given the go-ahead to completely remake the failing school into the school of their dreams! UNFORTUNATELY, inspiring though this drama may be, this whole story is fictitious and is of limited value to the average parent of a child attending a failing school. Although, as I mentioned earlier, failing schools do have "turn-around" committees (usually led and dominated by well-paid educrats instead of the parents in the community) there is no mechanism, or procedure in the law in any state that I know of, for an angry crusading parent like Jaime to un-unionize a public school and turn it into a charter type operation. Too bad such a thing can't happen! But, meanwhile, a more realistic way might be to-

- Remake our child's failing elementary or middle school (I don't think this is going to work for high schools) like Principal David Nixon did when he took over John Calhoun Elementary School in Calhoun Hills, South Carolina. This crusading educator, whose story has been featured in "Newsweek Magazine", took over as Principal of this hellhole of a school in 2006. When Dave arrived he found the school in utter chaos, ninety percent of the students came from families living below the poverty line and 226 kids per year (out of a school population of only 250) were regular visitors to the principal's office where they were getting suspended or expelled! The violence at John Calhoun was so bad that teachers there themselves were quitting, pulling their own kids out, and leaving the district. Parent apathy- most likely stemming from parent hopelessness- was so bad that at Dave's first Parent- Teachers meeting only a dozen parents showed up. Our young Principal was literally at his wit's end as to how he could turn the situation around the first few weeks after his arrival.

Luckily for Dave, AND JOHN CALHOUN ELEMENTARY, he found the solution to all their problems in a dusty old file cabinet that had been locked up for years. In the cabinet he found a TWO FOOT LONG WOODEN PADDLE, its handle rapped in duck tape, somewhat worn by years of age and use. Being a thoroughly modern 21st century man he certainly had his doubts about bringing this archaic implement back into use, but when a distraught father with an uncontrollable son told him, "I want to give you authority to whip my son's butt", a light bulb went off in his head! What Dave did next was positively revolutionary. After getting the local school board's approval that he could do so, he sent out a letter to all the parents that he was re-instating CORPORAL PUNISHMENT at John Calhoun effective immediately. It turns out, surprisingly, that he could do this, as corporal punishment for students is STILL LEGAL for elementary and middle school disciplinary purposes both in South Carolina and in twenty other states. In his letter Dave let the kids' parents know that this big change was occurring, and informed them that if they were not in agreement with this, that the school board would let them move their child to a neighboring school where corporal punishment wouldn't be practiced. Again, to Dave's immense shock, only a handful of the beleaguered parents took him up on the offer to move their kids! Instead the parents of about 240 out of the 250 students basically said, "Hey, what do we got to lose, let's give it a try." So our young Principal brought back the disciplinary practices of a by-gone era. How does it work?

Now, prominently displayed behind Dave's principal's desk, hangs the wooden paddle in plain sight of all students called to the office. When a kid is brought in for a "major offence" such as fighting or stealing he is told to place both of his hands on the seat of a leather chair in front of him and brace for what Nixon calls "a whippin'". Before he begins, though, he sits the child down for a quiet talk about why he, or she, is in trouble. He tries to determine if a deeper issue, such as a problem at home, might warrant a meeting with a counselor. If the child shows remorse, Nixon will often send him or her back to class without a spanking. Otherwise, he makes sure that he is calm, and he makes sure that his elbow is still. Then he delivers "three licks" to the child's rear end. If the child is a girl, then a female administrator does it. Some of the kids cry. Some are silent. Some want a hug. And after the child has been sent back to class, still stinging, Nixon sits alone in his office thinking about what the child has done, and how he himself has responded. Practical Dave, who was a successful farmer before he became an educator, argues that his unusual disciplinary practices have had several advantages. "What are we here to do?" Nixon says. "We're here to educate. Before, when we suspended students they were out of the classroom and missing out on their education for days and days at a time. This caused them to fall further behind in their studies. Now, there's an immediate response to the kid's misbehavior, there's an immediate correction, and in less than fifteen minutes the child is right back in the classroom learning!" Humm…Very interesting. But how's this small, rural, Carolina school's field trip back into medieval times worked out as far as results go?

Very simple. THE SCHOOL HAS BEEN TURNED AROUND COMPLETELY! John Calhoun recently earned THREE statewide Palmetto awards, one for academic performance and two for overall improvement- the school's first such honors in its 35 year history. Referrals to the principal's office have declined by more than 80% and behavior problems at the school are now nearly non-existent! In addition, the parents, obviously benefiting from the enormous up swelling of hope that Dave has brought, now are almost unanimously involved in their kids' education and almost all of them are attending the parent-teacher conferences. Now that a few years have gone by since Mr. Paddle's made his return, its usage has become largely unnecessary due to the greatly improved behavior of Mr. Nixon's students. Weeks and months frequently pass by where it just hangs in back of Dave's desk gathering dust but every child called to his office-right up to the present day- still finds himself gazing up at it, and realizes that in this world, there surely are consequences for actions!

Are this innovative principal's methods the answer for all of our failing, out-of-control, elementary and middle schools? Probably not, as each school and every situation is somewhat different. But these are tools that might well work quite effectively with many of them. Remember too, that if we can gain control and respect over our younger students in the lower grades that it's going to carry over into better behavior in High School as well. When we look at the urban, inner city, dropout factory schools that are the primary focus of this book, we should bear in mind that they're far from being non-violent, peaceful places anyways! Some statistics even indicate that as many as one out of every nine teachers, at some point in their careers, will be assaulted by a student. Although at Williams I never was personally attacked by one of the kids, I did know several teachers who were. In the violent, chaotic schools that I have been describing, all that I'm saying is that maybe it would be good idea to HAVE THE STAFF BE IN CONTROL OF THE ASYLUM! In my own opinion many of our "wild west" inner city schools certainly could benefit from the application of Principal Nixon's methods. I'm sure that it would have been a big help at Williams! Now before dear reader you completely pooh pooh this idea, I'd like to share with you something that I read on a tiny piece of paper that I found with a footprint on it, stomped into a classroom floor one day last year. In beautiful, flowery writing (so I suspect that it must have been written by a young girl, probably somewhere around twelve years old) my heart twisted as a read the following poem:

SCREAMING TEACHER

I watched my teacher lose her mind.
Screaming in our classroom all the time!
All the bad kids did was cut up and play.

> So we learned nothing today.
> I wish someone would come
> Into our school-
> And make them behave,
> That would be cool! ☺

I wish I knew who the young lady was who wrote this poem, although we did have a few kids in that class who did seem to want an education, so I suppose that I could venture a guess. But I felt so sorry for her that I would gladly have donated my measly paycheck back to the city, if only a Dave Nixon type of principal could have come into Williams and restored order for her the way that he did down in Carolina! Remember the old commercial for the Negro College fund -"A mind is a terrible thing to waste?" How many beautiful young minds are we wasting today, because we're too namby-pamby to follow tried and true methods, and maintain adequate order and discipline in our schools? You tell me!

- WE CAN BRING VALUES BACK INTO OUR SCHOOLS! After the spate of school shootings that occurred during the past year while I've been writing this book, culminating in the incident where a five-year- old kindergartener in Tennessee shot a gun out of his backpack, I've come to realize that just as we can't SPEND OUR WAY out of our educational problems; neither can we substantially improve the caliber of our children's education without ADDRESSING THE MORAL COMPONENT. The blueprint for the effective academic classroom REQUIRES respect for the teacher (learned in early childhood as respect for adults) and respect and kindly feelings towards one's fellow students. Otherwise, the whole classroom model simply ceases to work! You can set your academic standards higher, or, you can set them lower; either way nothing significant can be accomplished with disrespectful, fighting kids. The people running the successful charter schools that we've been talking about know this. Stick-to-it ness, perseverance, respect while being corrected, CHARACTER TRAITS, are absolutely critical to success in the classroom. Barbara Ruggereo, principal of the extremely effective Children's Community School here in town, knows that. In a radio interview this year she explained that the children are

GRADED on their character traits and classroom behavior in every report card sent home, and that this is one subject that is discussed with each child's parents at every parent-teacher conference throughout the year. The Kip Academy system, in addition to never letting a kid fall significantly behind his classroom peers, also places a high emphasis on the student's character in their grading system. The Kip Academies are among the most successful charter schools in America today. They started out with only one school a few years back, but now have eighty-two throughout the country! Children at these schools who fall too far behind are assigned personal tutors. These charters have found that a kid who's fallen behind academically can usually (often with extra help) catch up, but a rebellious, disrespectful boy or girl is DEFINITELY IN BIG TROUBLE!

But how can we instill these positive character traits into our young people? I was shocked when I starting working at Williams, and I went to the school library, and was unable to find the Bible, the Torah, or even the Quran! When I asked the school librarian why those books were unavailable she said to me, "Well, you know Mr. Shine there is a separation between church and state." Heck, these works should be available to the students if only for their literary content! In the same library all kinds of picture books showing the human anatomy, almost to a pornographic degree were totally available, but heaven forbid that any kid would pick up a Bible! I agree with Texas governor Rick Perry on this one. He said, "In this country we have freedom OF religion, but that doesn't mean that we should have freedom FROM religion." Absolutely. Yes, they should have learned it at home, but if they haven't (and believe me many of them didn't) then it's up to us to teach them the basic moral standards of our American Judeo-Christian culture. And by the way, we're not really offending anyone on this, as these standards are quite consistent with the standards of Buddhism, Islam and even Jeremy Bentham's Utilitarianism. We can't have a generation of young savages rampaging through our school's hallways and expect any kind of meaningful learning to be occurring. Although we can't completely blame the kids for getting the wrong idea, as they've been raised by TV and the internet in this celebrity-obsessed, steroid sports-soaked "Win at all costs" environment, but we definitely do them no favors by letting them grow up with that type of mentality. We must change the attitude that so many of them have that "It's all about me, *uck everybody else"; otherwise we can turn our schools into fortresses with bullet-proof glass in every window and metal detectors at every door, and they will only be spanking new palaces of violence where our disconsolate children remain imprisoned. If, because of the metal detectors, they can't smuggle in guns to shoot each other, they'll stab each other with sharpened pencils. Heck, I've seen them do it!

- DIFFERENT STROKES FOR DIFFERENT FOLKS! Back in the 60's we used to say that. We should recognize that the classroom setting isn't the most appropriate one for each and every student. Functioning successfully in a teacher-led, traditional classroom, requires (as I just described in the previous section) a level of maturity, together with moral character and social skills, that some of our children today, unfortunately do not have. Insisting that these anti- authority, misbehaving, wild kids remain in the classroom with the rest of our children, is nothing more than a recipe for harm for both the wild kids and the good kids too. As a teacher known only as "Steve" who teaches at Crosley High here in my city (where my Williams students go when they graduate) posted on the web recently," This city is allowing 300 pupils at Crosley to destroy the only chance that the other 1,200 other learners have to succeed. I teach here. I see it every day." I'm sure that Steve, as well as hundreds of thousands of other teachers throughout America, will agree with me when I say "Pull those impossible kids right out of the classroom!" Luckily for us this is the $21^{st\ century}$ and there's an alternative for those excluded children. GIVE THAT KID A COMPUTER! I've mentioned before how much the students loved the computerized smart boards that the city put in, and how it was a struggle to keep the kids away from them, well they love regular computers just as much! As Pink Floyd said in their "Brick in the Wall" album, "Teacher, leave them kids alone!" For some kids, that may be best, to let them learn on computers at their own pace.

Speaking of computers, dear reader, do yourself a favor and go on You Tube and watch Suli Break's brilliant video "Why I Hate School but I Love Education" that has already received four million views. Suli points out that many, if not most, of the outrageously successful people in America today (and indeed throughout history) ARE NOT college graduates! He, and many of our truly intelligent, iconoclastic young people nowadays, see our schools as places of blind regimentation and regurgitation of useless facts, instead of being boot camps of the mind, where young brains are strengthened and taught HOW TO THINK. To quote Suli, "Education is the key, but school is the lock." He says that if you're not building your own dream then you're working to build someone else's! But whether you have a brilliant young mind like Suli's (or Bill Gates) or are, instead, just a wiseacre young know-it-all ghetto kid who doesn't want to sit there and listen to some fat gray haired old white guy in a suit and tie bloviate all day long; I can see, in your future, schools with cavernous areas of computer labs for you, where you can research and learn at your own speed.

In the forward thinking suburban towns of my admittedly quite progressive state some of the school districts are already beginning to take this enlightened road. In the small towns immediately to the North and East of my city hundreds of I-Pads have been passed out to the students and MIRACLES have begun to occur! These I-Pads, with their interactive textbooks and 3D pictures and illustrations, come with 20,000 different educational applications pre-installed. Gail Gray, a kindergarten teacher in one of our neighboring towns, is finding them a Godsend when it comes to teaching her little children their handwriting skills. Handwriting takes a lot of time, repetition, and practice. She said on pen and paper she can get a kindergarten student to focus for an average of 20 minutes. On the Ipad the child can focus on the same handwriting exercise for about 40 minutes. Practicing handwriting is always frustrating, she said, with the average student having to practice it 24 times before learning it correctly. With the number of students in her class, she simply couldn't focus on one student for that long, but students are always motivated to use their Ipads. The students get the repetition and feedback, with the computer praising the child for a job well done or telling him or her to try again. "It answers all my prayers," Gray said.

In another neighboring suburb, a pilot computerized learning program called "Pathways" is being implemented for kids who haven't done well in the traditional classroom setting. In a local newspaper article about "Pathways", student Jonathan Rodriguez admitting to getting all excited when the computer rewarded him with a gold star for completing another unit of his math course. "I wish I had this for all my classes" said Rodriguez, "I get pretty into it sometimes."

Jonathan's teacher, Cheryl French, said in the same article, "How cool is it to see high school kids so excited about their progress." With the computer courses students don't have to sit through hours of lectures on material they've already mastered. Positive feedback from the computer and progress reports help to motivate students. The program breaks down each step of the problems, showing how to solve them and testing comprehension each step of the way. A lot of the questions are multiple choice, but students also have to respond to written prompts, write research papers and complete projects for many of the courses. Although students work independently through the lessons, their teachers are still available at a moment's notice to answer any questions.

Ms. French says that the self-paced learning program on the computer limits the amount of down time when students might OTHERWISE get bored, distracted and act out. The computerized learning courses are designed to take 60 to 75 hours to complete and are aligned with common core standards. Although this coursework is just as difficult as the materials taught in the regular classrooms, the kids participating in the program tell their teachers that they find it more interesting and that they like it better. Unlike traditional classes, students are allowed to listen to music and chat with each other as they work!

According to the administration, not only are the students involved in "Pathways" making rapid academic progress, but that many kids who have previously DROPPED OUT of school are now clamoring to come BACK TO SCHOOL, if only that they could be allowed to participate in this new program. As a matter of fact, a waiting list has been established!

Furthermore, the way that this program has been designed, it allows students to rotate seamlessly between mainstream classes and Pathways. If a student falls behind in a regular class, for example, they might spend a few weeks reviewing material in the computer course before returning to the regular classroom. Teachers, from their master computer servers, can track students' progress and see how much time they have spent on each section. They can also see where, in the coursework, that the student is having trouble or getting bogged down, and can then go down to the kid's computer workstation and offer them extra help. Progress reports are mailed home weekly to the student's parents.

Talking about Pathways, teacher Cheryl French says, "It meets the needs of all students, no matter where they are." Which is, by the way, totally the opposite of the traditional classroom model that sacrifices the needs of each individual student, while trying to meet the needs of the larger group of students in the aggregate! Let's face it; group learning may not be for everyone. For both the slow learners who can't keep up with the rest of the class (and who become frustrated and then become disruptive students), and for the young geniuses, who are bored and slowed down by classmates (and who like Bill Gates, may drop out) what's wrong with individualized- often computerized- learning? Why have we, as a society, been so slow on picking up on these new technologies, which we ourselves here in America, have invented? Are we really as concerned, as we say we are, about ALL our children being given the best opportunities to learn? Or are we more concerned about job security for teachers?

- WE CAN STOP THINKING OF ALL OF OUR HIGH SCHOOLS AS COLLEGE PREPARATORY ACADAMIES! As Suli Breaks (and the Center for College Affordability and Productivity) have pointed out, the idea that "every kid should go to college" is a totally failed fantasy. I've said before that the statistics from this Center indicate, according to the 2010 census, HALF of ALL COLLEGE GRADUATES (not just recent graduates either) are either unemployed, or are working at jobs that they didn't have to go to college for. And these figures aren't even taking into account the fact that half of all the students who begin college never graduate anyways! Where do you think those young people are working? Yet, every single High School in this country constantly brags about the percentage of their graduates going on to college; as if that was some kind of proof that that particular High School was doing a fantastic job! Many "good" ones claim that 90% or more of their graduates go on to college. So what? Shouldn't we be preparing our high school students for life, INSTEAD OF for college? We march all of our young people in this country, like a bunch of lemmings, down a narrow gangplank into colleges regardless of whether or not this is in every kid's best interest! Once again we foolishly look at everyone as if they were identical and don't see them as unique individuals. Many, if not an absolute majority (especially among the 50% who drop out of college along the way), will end up with NOTHING from their "you must go to college" adventure besides an enormous student loan and a minimum wage job in retail!

I've mentioned that my city has recently opened a second vocational high school. Although this is good, in my opinion, this is nothing but a very tepid start towards what needs to be done. At the risk of sounding like an old fogy, I remember that when I was going to high school back in the 60's, only ONE THIRD of the kids were in what was called the "college prep" program. TWO THIRDS of the students then were in what were called "general studies" or "business/vocational." I think that percentages along those lines would BETTER MEET THE NEEDS of our children now a days too!

Our high schools need to be totally revamped and drastically moved away from the academically difficult, "we're preparing all the students for college" model and transformed into vocational centers where kids are studying computer science, electronics, carpentry, masonry, beauty science, retail management and so on ad infinitum. Apprenticeship programs (with local manufacturing companies, contractors or business establishments) can be an integral part of this.

Olympic High School, in Charlotte North Carolina, is already experimenting with this. Following the European apprenticeship model, students at career academies within the school are being pared with companies like Bosch, Siemans, and Duke Energy where they spend much of their school day working with real life supervisors and learning a real life trade. These young kids are training for skilled jobs that may well be more meaningful (and more lucrative) than the jobs that they might have obtained after having earned a four- year degree. And promising students can start earning right away-sometimes while they're still in high school-and later don't have to load themselves down with crushing college student loan debts. As a matter of fact, the companies mentioned will often pay the community college tuition for apprentices whose work pleases them and whom they are later planning to hire!

Michael Realon, Olympic High's liaison to the manufacturing community, explained how this program works in a recent "Mcclatchey" newspaper article. Students, when they first come into this vocational high school, are given online assessments of their skills and interests giving them a list of their 20 best career "matches." Realon tells them, "It's like eHarmony. We're going to connect you to your soul-mate career that will make you happy." When he first meets many of the kids, Mike claims that they're kind of "down in the dumps" after years and years of failure in their previous academically-oriented schooling, but he cheers them up by telling them, "All that testing stuff and all that rote memorization stuff is not going to help you out in the real world." Instead, he assures them, he's more concerned with them pleasing their on-the-job supervisors out on their work sites, and having them fit well into the corporate cultures of the companies that may, one day, hire them. As the students do well working on the job sites, and are learning the ropes of careers in which they're interested, their spirits improve and behavior problems become almost non-existent!

Imagine what a happy place our high schools would be if all the students were studying things that they WANTED TO STUDY and if the HEAVY CROSS of the unnecessary academic studies could be removed from the shoulders of the vast majority of students who were now on a vocationally-orientated trajectory?

And don't worry, if certain math or other academic skills are genuinely needed by the trade school kids- BELIEVE YOU ME-THEY WILL INDEED LEARN THEM. As any teacher that you've ever met will gladly tell you, WHERE INTEREST IS- LEARNING FOLLOWS CLOSELY BEHIND!

Finally, let's keep in mind, that under the current system, the way we do it now, vast numbers of our high school graduates (and yeah, this helps boost the educrats' statistics) are going to be going on to get the practical, nuts and bolts vocational training that I've been talking about, by attending community colleges or technical schools. And that this post-high school schooling isn't cheap! So why not give their parents (who are also the beleaguered taxpayers paying for our schools) a break by putting their tax dollars to good use by providing a practical, worthwhile education for their kids INSIDE our public high schools? It would save time, money, and endless frustration!

- We can dramatically INCREASE THE TIME, BOTH IN SCHOOL DAYS AND IN SCHOOL HOURS that our children spend in their classrooms! You will search in vain, dear reader, to find any other workplace in America where the cadences and rhythms of the job have remained virtually unchanged since the 18th and 19th centuries. Kids in our country still go to school but 180 days a year and only six hours a day! Children are generally done with school by 2:30 in the afternoon. If we take the education of our young people seriously why, may I ask, do we conduct it like a part-time job?

I'm afraid to say that it all harkens back to Colonial (and even pre-Colonial) times when the academic day, and the academic year, were established. Back in those by-gone times the primary purpose of a child was very different than it is today. Now-a-days we see that the main purpose of childhood is to get a good education so as to prepare for adult life. But way back then, they thought that the main purpose of a child was to help on the family farm! That's why kids got the summer off- that was the busiest time of year on the farm. Schools were closed early in the afternoon, as the children were expected to come home and help with chores before darkness fell. It wasn't at all unusual for kids to be hired out to other farmers (or storekeepers in the village) during the afternoon, when they weren't enough chores on the farm to keep them busy; so they could bring in additional revenue for the family. Going to school was considered a luxury; it was almost looked on as an after-thought! Heck, most kids never even went to high school. If our farm boys back then made it to 7th or 8th grade and learned, readin' and writin' and 'rithmatic that was considered just fine. Most of the girls didn't even make it that far; their educations were considered completely adequate if they could just learn how to sew and can vegetables!

But why, oh why, are these schedules still in effect today- in the 21st century?? The Egyptians could never have been expected to build the pyramids working six- hour days, could they? And what kind of homes are we sending these children home to in the early afternoons? Empty ones basically! Census statistics show that 60% of all families have TWO working parents (or in the ghettos of our inner-cities TWO partying parents) so nobody's home when our kids get there anyways. Instead of learning, what are these kids doing during these long afternoons until they meet up with their parents? From what the kids at Williams told me, most likely they're playing video games, posting stuff on Facebook, or yakking on the 'phone!

Realizing that usually, if you want to accomplish more, you have to work more, the charter schools that I've been talking about ALREADY HAVE drastically extended the lengths of their school days and their school years. The Children's Community School here in my city, for example, has a 190-day school year and the kids go there from 7:30 am to 5 pm.

Some public schools that are truly serious about improving student results have begun to move in this direction as well. Take Hilton Elementary School in Baltimore Maryland; there the school day lasts nearly ten hours but includes ample time for the students to eat, exercise, and flex their creative juices while still learning core subjects like math and English. After 3 pm a community group comes in and offers the kids one-on-one mentoring in subjects as diverse as dance, chess, photography, gardening, and sign language. The extended schedule matches the work schedules of most parents and also helps the school tap into available free time of the mentors, who may be busy with regular jobs earlier in the day. Local musicians like mentoring later in the day (maybe after late night gigs), and software designers come into the school when their companies let them do some community volunteer work during the afternoons. Athletes from local sports teams have been known to stop by as well. Supplementing the school day with more opportunities for learning- whether it be though expanded hours or after-school and summer programs- can help close the achievement gap that we've been speaking about. Low- income students can get the music lessons, or other much longed for "hobby" type lessons, RIGHT IN THE SCHOOL SETTING, that the rich kids' families are paying for them to receive privately after school. In my mind this sure beats having the kid sit home alone, probably posting bullying posts about fellow classmates on Facebook!

I know that our teachers (and their unions), who dearly love their long summer vacations and their short workdays during the rest of the year are going to hate me, but we immediately have to do something about the pathetically short amount of time that our kids are spending in school. In this 21st century, the great world power that's expected to be our biggest rival is China. There, children attend school from 6 am to 6 pm. They are allotted two hours each day during that period for eating and exercise, but how are we ever to compete with our kids still following the part-time farm kids schedule of the 18th century? Only when our teachers and students begin to see and work at education like a fulltime job, and start putting into their jobs the kind of effort that the rest of us put into our jobs, will we begin to experience the joy of our system starting to hit on all cylinders. TO GET FULL TIME RESULTS, WE'RE GOING TO HAVE TO HAVE FULL TIME WORK!

- WE CAN GET THE WORST TEACHERS OUT OF OUR CHILDREN'S CLASSROOMS. This isn't going to be easy one to accomplish, the teachers' unions can be expected to fight us tooth and nail, but it has to be done anyways! As in other professions, there are a certain number of neer-do-wells, screw-ups, and lazy boneses who have, unfortunately, gone into teaching; but the problem is that WE CAN'T GET RID OF THESE PEOPLE. Some studies have indicated that as many as fifty percent of all young teachers, once they're certified, drop out of teaching within the first five years; what do I have to say about that? It reminds me of the old joke that we used to tell back in the day: "What do you call 1,000 lawyers drown at the bottom of the ocean?" Answer: "A good start!" Yeah, a large number of individuals, realizing that they don't have what it takes, voluntarily remove themselves from the classroom (especially in the first years-their baptism of fire), but that number isn't quite enough to accomplish our purpose of providing every single student with a truly high-quality teacher. Educational reformers have speculated that if we could just get the BOTTOM PERFORMING SIX PERCENT of our teachers to pack it in, our country's educational results could match Finland's.

I mentioned in the last chapter the problems that are entailed whenever the administration decides that a teacher has to be let go. I talked about the "rubber rooms" where hundreds of teachers who were accused of malfeasance or incompetence collected paychecks for up to eighteen months while their cases slowly percolated through the system. How experts have determined that the total costs involved in getting rid of JUST ONE TEACHER average over $300,000!

A good example of what happens when the administration gets SERIOUS ABOUT REMOVING BAD TEACHERS is the story of School Chancellor Michelle Rhee in Washington, DC. This brave, crusading woman received high praise from Oprah Winfrey when she took on the Herculean task of reforming our nation's capital's public school system. A system that is, by the way, one of the worst ones in the country. Heck, President Obama wouldn't even send his own girls there! Chancellor Rhee, when she came into office, noticed an enormous DISCONNECT. Although only 8% of the district's students were performing at grade level, 95% of all the teachers had either "good" or "excellent" evaluations!

She asked herself, "How can the final product be so bad, if the workers are doing such an excellent job?" She realized (as we've pointed out before) that the teacher's evaluations on file were far from being objective, and that cronyism and friendly principals, accounted for the vast majority of the reports that she was reading. WHETHER THE TEACHER'S STUDENTS WERE MAKING PROGRESS OR NOT generally wasn't a major factor in the evaluations!

So Chancellor Rhee began taking a closer look at her teachers, and began to weed out the good sheep from the goats. She FIRED over one thousand teachers and, of course, test scores in the district began to improve dramatically. As might have been expected, the educational blob- the teachers' unions and their allies- struck back with a vengeance! Within a couple of years they managed to drum her out of office and to roll back all of her reforms. Sadly, the district's test scores have resumed their submarine slide towards the ocean's floor, but still Chancellor Rhee has shown us what bravery and commonsense can accomplish if only given half a chance.

To further illustrate how horrible some teachers can be, you may recall that I mentioned that back in the 70's I had been a state social worker investigating allegations of child abuse and neglect. As many of these reports came in after 9-5, I volunteered to work odd hours- nights and weekends- for a government sponsored service called "Careline" so as to go out there and investigate these cases promptly. A large number of referrals came in from teachers, but what shocked me was that in the four years I did this work, only a handful of them were willing to meet with me AFTER REGULAR SCHOOL DAY HOURS! This created a big problem; as due to my humongous caseload my pre-set appointment schedule was usually booked pretty solid, so that when teachers REFUSED TO STAY AFTER SCHOOL TO MEET WITH ME IN THE AFTERNOON, I was FORCED TO POSTPONE my one-on-one interview with the teacher that usually was the best way to begin such an investigation. Sometimes our investigations were DELAYED FOR WEEKS AT A TIME while I tried to juggle my appointment book to work around teachers "only during the school day" schedule! Other caseworkers complained to me that they had had the same problem. What kind of people, or should I say hypocrites, are these who claim to be so concerned about the well-being of the young souls in their charge, but then are unwilling to give up even a few minutes of their free time to speak with State-mandated investigators about allegations of abuse or neglect that they, themselves, had made? They don't sound like professionals to me, THEY SOUND LIKE CLOCK-WATCHERS!

I wonder if the general public knows that when their child's teacher meets with them in the evening on parent-teacher nights that that teacher is given compensatory time off during the day? Or, is as more typical, the school day itself is shortened (so your child's learning is cut short) to make up for the time the teacher must spend with the parents? Humm… No wonder Cameron Diaz' character, the slacker teacher, said in the movie "Bad Teacher", "Of course I became a teacher, short hours, long summer vacations, good pay, what's not to like?" She portrayed a hooker-type teacher in that film that drove teenaged boys into conniptions.

But prevalent as these abominations are in our schools they're the EXACT OPPOSITE of the way a teacher should be. We've discussed (and lauded) good teachers in this book and they too are, thankfully, quite prevalent as well. A good teacher is what the Japanese call a sensei, in other words a master. I even wrote a poem about it:

TEACHER AS SENSEI

Teachers must first inspire a certain amount of fear in their students. Without this they can't even teach what 2 plus 2 is….

> They won't listen!
> Learning comes from listening;
> And no one listens to someone
> They don't first fear and respect.
> The sensei is first of all a master!

Our teachers should be senseies, not clock- watchers. Governor Malloy in my state, along with other governors as well, has begun to try and push towards more objective teacher performance evaluations, and to re-open the centuries old concept of locked in teacher tenure, but, as I've noted; due to the complexity of putting these changes into effect (not to mention the enormous push-back from the teachers' unions) weeding out all our ineffective teachers probably isn't going to be something that we'll be celebrating anytime soon. In the meanwhile, all I care to say to those slackers who've gone into teaching for the same reasons as Cameron Diaz' character did in "Bad Teacher" are five words: GET OUT OF THE PROFESSION! This advice applies as well to those teachers who were once effective, but have lost their "Mojo", have been marinating in the schools for many years and who will, if only they'd be honest with themselves, admit that now they're just in it for the short, convenient hours and the money. Not to worry, there are plenty of part-time jobs in retail for minimalists like you at places like Walmart and Starbucks. At those jobs you can punch YOUR TIMECLOCKS to your heart's content, fly out the exits every day as the minute hand hits the prick of the hour, and the closing bell starts to ring. And the good news is that you won't be short-changing our precious children and messing up their futures with your slacker, loser ways either!

- WE CAN EMBRACE AN EDUCATIONAL VOUCHER SYSTEM FOR OUR CHILDREN. Especially in districts where more than half of the public schools are failing (like my city) we can give the kids' parents vouchers to pay for their children to attend charter schools. It doesn't really matter if these private schools are religious (parochial) or secular, in most cases as we've shown previously, the students are going to get a far superior education there than they're going to be getting in the existing public schools. Instead of cutting checks payable to the parents, the school board should direct pay the charter school in question for that child's tuition. MONEY SHOULD FOLLOW THE CHILD. In most instances only 75% of what is spent for public school education needs to be paid to the charter school (that's what most charter schools seem to accept) so the taxpayers would get a well-deserved break on this new program as well! The reason for this is that the charter school's costs, despite their longer hours and extended school years, are far lower than the public schools as they're almost always non-union. They also don't need to be located in the showy, Taj Mahal type edifices that our politicians love to cut the ribbons for every year! So these schools can MAKE MONEY despite the fact that per pupil expenditures are much cheaper. The City of New Orleans has already started a program along these lines due to the fact that many of their public schools were put out of commission by hurricane Katrina. Because they couldn't get them up and running for the beginning of the school year, the city offered vouchers for parents to put their kids into charter schools. Now that the city schools have finally been repaired, the kids (and their parents) have found that they like the charter schools so much that the vast majority doesn't want to come back! New Orleans is now the only major city in the country where more students are attending charter schools than are attending public, AND TEST SCORES ARE BEGINNING TO RISE!

Competition is good, that's how things improve and are made better. I'm sure that if we had a voucher system many of our public schools, in their struggle to retain students, would become immensely more effective and everyone would benefit. I'm not counting our public school teachers out by a long shot! Still, I wouldn't be at all surprised, that- like in New Orleans- many of our worst public schools would empty out, leaving city administrations with scores of vacant buildings that they haven't the slightest idea of what to do with. I've got an idea: since our cities seem to love these places so much, turn them into low-income section 8 housing, soup kitchens, homeless shelters, halfway houses, alternative correctional facilities and so forth. Let's not just sell them off for a dollar or two apiece (as my city was wont to do in the past), so that private developers can make a fortune out of what taxpayers have paid for with their hard-earned money!

- GIVE OUR KIDS CONTINUITY IN THEIR EDUCATION. Inner- city parents move around a lot. For whatever reason, whether it's because families are being evicted, or living conditions change, it's not uncommon for a child from this milieu to live at two or three different addresses in the course of one academic year. At Williams, I personally met several kids who had been bounced around to all three of our city's middle schools within the course of one school year! They stayed in our city, but because their parents moved them across district lines, they were forced to re-adapt to a new educational surrounding every few months. Understandably, these children struggled mightily just to keep up with their peers! BUT WHY SHOULD CHILDREN BE MADE TO SUFFER FOR THE NEGLIGENCE OF THEIR PARENTS? This doesn't happen at the charter schools. In those schools, no matter where the kid is living (so long as it's in the same city) he remains in the same classroom with the same teacher. Since 95% of our children in the cities are bused to school anyways, what difference does it make as to where exactly that student lives? We should start running our educational system for the convenience and benefit or THE STUDENTS and not for the ease and convenience of the EDUCRATS with their inflexible rules, regulations and "district lines!"

- WE CAN DEMAND THAT OUR SCHOOLS PRODUCE BETTER STUDENTS, NOT JUST BETTER TEST TAKERS! "Teaching to the test" has become a way of life in our public schools! I talked about the principal who was more concerned about whether or not a student had finished his CMT as opposed to whether he had assaulted another student, but this is, I'm afraid to say, par for the course in our current educational system. As the higher up educrats' careers rise and fall on the numbers generated by standardized testing, maybe it's understandable that raising those tests results- by hook or crook- is becoming the primary focus of every administrator. Whether or not this should be the biggest priority for the student is another matter! I personally witnessed teachers, wasting weeks and even months of the precious little academic time that we had, while they desperately coached the kids in test-taking skills starting in September (the CMTs were in April), and putting the most important aspects of their subjects on the back burner. The teachers themselves are rightly complaining that they're being overwhelmed with all the testing and the endless prep work that the administrators mandate.

I'm not the only one who sees a problem with this. Diane Ravitch Ph.D, a research professor of education at New York University and author of the book "Reign of Error", writes that "Schools are under so much pressure to get students to pass that most of the school day is spent teaching to the test. Subjects that don't appear on the tests- art, foreign languages, even science and history- are being dropped from the curriculum." The result, says journalist Paul Tough, author of the book "How Children Succeed", is that we're producing many grads that are great test takers but not great learners. "Students don't know how to deal well with confrontation, bounce back from defeat, see two different sides of a problem," he says, "things that are essential not just in adulthood but in continuing your education past high school. It turns out the students who are most likely to graduate from college aren't necessarily the ones who do best on the standardized tests, but the ones who are able to develop these other qualities."

Abby Cohen, a fifty year old, long-time teacher from Newton, Mass., when interviewed on this subject by "Parade" magazine stated, "I think the biggest crime is that teaching has turned to focus on the tests, rather than the tests being a tool that help you understand. All the teaching and learning is on the subject being tested." Cohen worries that her daughter, Isabel, who is starting her senior year, hasn't gotten as much real learning as she could have from her teachers due to their narrow-minded focus on the testing, and the testing alone. "You have to ask how much you're straight-jacketing the teachers," Cohen said.

Again, if we looked upon our schools as being training grounds for success in adult life as a whole, rather than just as being college-prep incubation academies, the raw testing scores of each and every student wouldn't carry the earthshaking ramifications that they do now, under the present flawed system. I think that we're evaluating our schools, teachers, and administrators in a completely wrong manner. Maybe, what we should be doing is generating statistics about how well our young people are doing-say- five years after they graduate from high school. Are they employed? Does that job pay a living wage? Are they happy in their work? Schools whose graduates score well on those types of surveys are schools, that we can be pretty sure are productive and are "performing well." On the other hand, schools where large numbers of the kids don't even graduate, and who, even when they do graduate, indicate on the five-year thereafter surveys that they are unemployed, or employed only at minimum wage jobs that they hate, should be designated "failing schools"- REGARDLESS OF WHAT THE RAW SCORES MAY SHOW. This would be a fairer and far more effective measuring tool for use in evaluating how our schools (and their teachers and administrators) are performing as opposed as to how their students do ON SOME STUPID, ARBITRARY TEST!

- WE CAN BRING BACK RECESS, OR AT LEAST DAILY, MANDATORY PHYSICAL ACTIVITY FOR ALL OUR KIDS. I agree with Michelle Obama on this one, we've got to get our children moving again. And this doesn't just mean trouping classrooms of them down to the gym, like I witnessed at Williams, where the vast majority stand around with their hands in their pockets as they watch the more athletically-gifted kids play basketball! EACH AND EVERY CHILD SHOULD PARTICIPATE! Shockingly, today only nine states require recess in elementary schools, so many of our kids are getting no exercise whatsoever. I've spoken anecdotally about how fidgety the kids were, and how they could hardly sit in their seats and pay attention to their lessons (especially when they came back upstairs from their nearly worthless phys. ed. classes), but now empirical evidence is being published showing just how important physical exercise really is.

Doctor Robert Murray, a pediatrician and a fellow at the American Academy of Pediatrics, also interviewed by "Parade" magazine stated that, "Studies show that daily physical activity allows students to perform at their optimum." He added "It's counter-productive to push for more academic time without also allowing regular breaks to process what they've learned. That's exactly what recess represents." As the science is now somewhat settled on this, First Lady Michelle Obama is asking all school administrators to schedule in at least 60 minutes of physical activity into each school child's day.

Our ancestors were well aware of this intimate mind/body connection. When I was young I was taught that the ancient Greeks and Romans, in educating their young men, went by the motto, "A SOUND MIND IN A SOUND BODY." We, unfortunately in this country, have pulled a 180 degree reversal in the opposite (wrong) direction from that ideal. Instead, we're producing a generation of video game-obsessed, pathologically obese couch potatoes!

Let's just look at the numbers from one of our States as an example. In Georgia, Department of Public Health Commissioner Brenda Fitzgerald reported that only sixteen percent of her state's current students could pass the mandatory physical fitness tests that, only twenty years ago, eighty or ninety percent of the kids could easily pass! These tests measure flexibility, body/mass index, aerobic capacity (kids go for either a one-mile run or walk depending on their stamina) and the ability to do push-ups and curl-ups. Only one in five of the Georgia kids could, in this past year, pass ANY OF THESE TESTS! I think that we're fooling ourselves if we expect kids that are that far out-of-shape to be able to absorb their lessons as well as healthy kids can. The childhood obesity epidemic that is over-whelming America will, if unchecked, cause this current generation of our children to become the first in history who WILL DIE YOUNGER THAN THEIR PARENTS DO!

Luckily for us, the same technology that may have helped to create the problem can turn out to be a big part of the solution. A company called "KIDSFIT" has invented, and started to market, kinesthetic tables to replace traditional, static just "sit down in it', school desks! The way these work is that they are similar to elliptical machines, the child stands at them and, with their feet on the pedals, can walk or run while reading, listening or testing. In front of the child is a desk-like surface that can be used for writing, holding a book, or just for the kid to rest his elbows. These contraptions are larger and taller than normal school desks and, unfortunately, are somewhat expensive. They currently run almost $3,000 apiece! BUT KIDS LOVE THEM!

A close-by suburb of my city received a grant from the "Education Connection", a regional educational resource group for Litchfield County, to place these high-tech replacements for school desks into Fischer Elementary School where they're doing wonders for the kids' abilities to concentrate and to stay focused on their lessons; not to mention how much they're contributing to keeping these kids fit! According to an interview given to my local paper,

Lisa Daly, the grant coordinator for the suburb that put in these tables stated, "Younger kids can be so fidgety, the tables help them to release some of that energy so they can concentrate for longer periods of time."

In the same interview Fisher School Principal Phyllis Worhunsky said, "We want minds and bodies to be in the right place to learn. Studies have shown that doing something physical before completing a task helps with concentration, so if a student asks to use the table before a math test, that might help." Kinesthetic tables are especially good at helping kinesthetic learners, students who learn best through physically doing something rather than just listening or seeing. These tables allow learners to move while reading or writing, which helps them concentrate. The children at Fisher switch classrooms for math and language arts, giving all the students the opportunity to use the tables. Many teachers allow kids to run or walk at their "desks" during silent reading time.

Joan Zabek, a first grade teacher at Fisher, said she uses the tables to reward good behavior and to let the students release energy. "Some days, you can just tell who needs it," she said. "But it definitely works." Oliver Garceau, 5, and Colby Pronovost, 6, are both in Ms. Zabek's class. While the newspaper reporter was there they completed a spelling handout while at the tables pumping their legs. "It's like you're running in place!" Oliver told Alexa Gorman (the newspaper reporter). "Yeah, it's really fun," Colby said.

I wish the students who were bouncing around in their seats at Williams had had something like this! Again, I have only one question; why aren't we putting tables like this in ALL OF OUR CHILDRENS' elementary, middle- and even- high schools? We complain that our kids are "hyperactive" so what do we do about it? We zonk them out on meds! We can't ever seem to get them docile enough to keep their teachers happy. Talk about child abuse!

- WE CAN PUT CAMERAS IN ALL OF OUR SCHOOLS' CLASSROOMS. There are two reasons for this. Firstly, to help improve student behavior; you can't believe, dear reader, how many times when the staff informed kids' parents how horribly they were behaving in class, the parents informed us that there was no way that their "little angels" could have ever acted like that! Once in a blue moon, a parent of one of the monster kids would make a school visit and actually sit beside the offending student in the classroom. What do you think happened? You guessed it! The day that Mom or Dad (or grandma) was there, little Attila the Hun would behave like Pope Francis. The only thing many of these (usually rare) parental visits accomplished was to cause the teachers to lose credibility in the eyes of the parents. BUT IF WE HAD VIDEOS of the child's shenanigans the parents would've had to believe us! Having two-way mirrors built into the walls of the classroom so that the parents, while unobserved, could watch their kids in real-time would be another solution.

The second reason for the cameras though WOULD BE TO IMPROVE STAFF BEHAVIOR! I think that it was for fear of exposing the staff's misbehavior that the kids at Williams (and most other schools) were never allowed to take out their cell phones. I even witnessed cases where the kids took photos of embarrassing- at least to the staff-events and then the administration confiscated the phones and deleted the pictures! Among the things that the students could have taken pictures of were: substitute teachers sleeping, filing their nails or reading romance novels when they were supposed to be teaching the class, students being assaulted or bullied while staff turned a blind eye, certified teachers spending days upon days of class time letting their kids watch cartoons or the latest movie comedies, and also allowing sixth, seventh and eighth graders to spend entire class periods doodling or playing with coloring books! NO WONDER THE ADMINISTRATION WAS SO STRINGENT ABOUT NO ONE EVER USING A CAMERA IN THE CLASSROOM! We're putting video cameras on all of our students' school buses, so why not have them in their actual classes too? Isn't what (or what's not) going on in the classroom itself at least as important as what's happening on the ride back and forth to school? One would think so. Besides, a live feed from the teacher's class would be an invaluable help for the principal when it came time for that teacher's evaluation. Again, reality TV would be ten times more informative than pre-scheduled classroom visits that, I'm sure, even the worst teacher is totally prepared for. Why would our administrators oppose something like this?

- FINALLY, WE CAN DRASTICALLY INCREASE THE AMOUNT OF "BAD APPLE" KIDS EXPELLED FROM OUR PUBLIC SCHOOL SYSTEMS.

And I don't mean "suspended" either, I mean permanently EXPELLED! These juvenile delinquents cluttering up our classrooms, who are uninterested in learning, and whose disciplinary needs are monopolizing an unbelievable percentage of our teachers' scarce time, as they terrorize their fellow students, do not deserve to sit in the same classroom WITH YOUR CHILD! Keeping them "mainstreamed" as the educrats call it, does them no favor as they hate being in school anyway, and feel that their only purpose in being there (besides socializing with their friends), is to make their teachers' lives miserable. We are babysitting these kids, not teaching them! Meanwhile, when you have a sufficient quota of them in class- as is common in many inner-city schools- your own child, and his teacher, become so distracted that the learning process is almost completely disrupted! Why are we penalizing the majority who are there to learn, for the questionable benefit of this minority of kids whose so-called "right" to be mainstreamed has turned our public schools into war zones? Aren't we supposed to be pursuing "the greatest good for the greatest number?"

I'm not really sure what we should do with these educationally adverse, violent, disrespectful malcontents, whose hatred of any sort of authority is only matched by their self-obsession. That may well be the subject of another book. Maybe we can place them in correctional type schools; cinderblock barrack structures where they would spend 90% of their time learning how to behave and academics are only secondary, but that isn't my focus. I'm only saying that we've got to get them OUT OF THE CLASSROOMS THAT YOUR CHILD IS ATTENDING AND GET THEM OUT NOW!

After a great deal of study and personal experience, I've come to think of the educational system as a three-legged stool. We have the child, the child's parent(s), and the child's teacher, who's backed up by the school's administrators and the rest of the establishment. When we have a child, who's motivated and eager to learn, coming from a household where the parents value education and see it as the royal road for their child's future, combined with a teacher who loves children, is anxious to impart knowledge, and who sees their profession as a high, noble calling, we have a strong, sturdy stool and WE GET GREAT RESULTS!

On the other hand, when you have a child who looks upon school as an earlier form of prison (by the way many of these delinquents will indeed become jailbirds later when they grow up), coming from a permanent underclass household that's been on welfare for generations and hates authority, put into classrooms with clock-punching teachers who've completely given up on ever making a difference, then you'll have a rickety, piece of junk stool that'll collapse under a feather! YOU'LL HAVE A RECIPE FOR THE DROPOUT FACTORIES THAT WE'VE BEEN TALKING ABOUT IN THIS BOOK!

All of the suggestions that I've been highlighting are aimed at strengthening that educational system stool. These suggestions are NOT ALL INCLUSIVE, you too, my friend reader, may have others to add, but let me just stress this; A CHANGE HAS TO COME AND IT HAS TO COME FAST!

We, the parents and grandparents of the children in the public schools today, must immediately wrest control of this failing system from the entrenched bureaucracy currently running things. These educrats (as long as they get their counted-on annual raises) ARE QUITE HAPPY with the status quo and the glacial pace of change that we've been seeing. If we leave them in charge of things pretty soon it'll BE TOO LATE!

There's no way that America can long remain the preeminent, hegemonic, world-policeman Empire that we have now become, while we still have a failing school system half-rooted back in the 19th century! Heck, I don't even see how we could even be able to be ranked in the top tier of developed nations. We've got to be careful, we spend SO MUCH TIME NOW propagandizing our little ones with politically correct values, and SO LITTLE TIME teaching them math, reading, and science; that to me it's going to be quite questionable as to what these children are going to with this land of ours once they inherit it. Abraham Lincoln (who was largely self-educated) said, "The philosophy of the classroom in one generation will be the philosophy of the government in the next." So what will be our kids' philosophies twenty or thirty years from now? What will the government that they put into power look like? One thing I know, there's NO WAY AMERICA CAN BE A FIRST RATE COUNTRY WITH SECOND RATE SCHOOLS!

16

What You Can Do for Your Child

Recently, a fifteen- year old Pakistani girl named Malala was shot in the face and almost killed by the Taliban. Her crime? She wanted an education! Miraculously, she's survived and become an inspiration to boys and girls all over the world, kids who gladly face bullets to go to school. Hopefully the good kids here in America, YOUR KIDS, value education at least half as much as Malala does! What can we do to help them to learn? If you don't care where you're going, any road will take you there. But you've got to expect a lot of dead ends! Assuming that you do, however, want the best possible educational outcome for your child right now, in the present living under the seriously flawed educational system that we've been describing; what SPECIFICALLY can you do to insure that result? Albert Einstein once said, "I never teach my pupils. I only attempt to provide the conditions in which they can learn." So then, taking this wise man's advice as our starting point, what can we do to PROVIDE THE CONDITIONS that our children need to get the most out of what's out there right now? Here's a handy list:

1) IF YOU'RE A FATHER STAY IN YOUR CHILD'S LIFE! As I'm writing this last chapter of the book, my home-office window is open and I hear my neighbors' children playing outside on the lawn. They're two adorable little preschool girls, and I hear them calling out, again and again, as they run about and follow their father "Daddy, Daddy, DAAAAEEE!"

What love and inexpressible affection, longing and sweetness, I hear in their bird-like melodious chirps. I've come to realize that children need their fathers almost as MUCH AS THEY NEED OXOGEN! I fully understand that, unfortunately, there are many unwed mothers raising children alone, and that these single women are doing the best they can to raise their kids on their own; but the results aren't pretty. For example, the American Institutes for Research have found that 90% of ALL HOMELESS OR RUNAWAY CHILDREN came from fatherless households. They also found that 71% of high school dropouts and 63% of the youth who COMMITED SUICIDE did as well. Children who live in single-parent households are also 82% more likely to experience child poverty. Of course, people are individuals and you can't generalize, your fatherless child may well overcome the odds and become the next President Obama, but, nevertheless I'm a betting man and I'd rather run with the odds than to go against them. So, I'm going to stick by my initial advice: IF YOU'RE A FATHER STAY IN YOUR CHILD'S LIFE!

2) MAKE SURE THAT YOUR CHILD GETS A BREAKFAST IN THE MORNING BEFORE THE LEARNING DAY BEGINS. Of course we put fuel in our cars before we take them on a long trip, but are we making sure that our boys and girls are fueled up before they begin their morning studies? You'd probably be surprised to learn that, according to a 2011 study, although 77% of young children were getting breakfast every day, only 50% of middle-schoolers and just 36% of high schoolers ate a regular morning meal! Those statistics aren't nearly good enough for our elementary school kids and, as you can see, we've GOT A REAL PROBLEM with our older students. Apparently when our children get into the later grades they're probably feeling more rushed in the morning and they don't take time out to eat. Parents also are more inclined to be lax in their supervision of their older kids. THIS IS A MISTAKE. Interviewed in "Parade" magazine, nutrition researcher Gail Rampersaud of the University of Florida said, "Breakfast consumption improves cognitive function and is correlated with improved school attendance." In the same "Parade" article schools in Denver, Colorado reported drastic declines in student tardiness, and far fewer missed school days once a school breakfast program was established. Many schools now (including Williams where I worked) have established these breakfast programs but it's YOUR JOB, as a parent, to make sure that your child is participating in them or, if

they'd prefer, that they're eating a healthy breakfast at home. Either way, check up on your kid; check with the school and make sure he or she is really eating there- OTHERWISE DON'T LET THEM OUT THE DOOR WITHOUT A GOOD BREAKFAST!

3) MAKE SURE YOUR CHILD GETS A GOOD NIGHT'S SLEEP BEFORE A SCHOOL DAY. Remember what we learned from Doctor Brad Wolgast back in Chapter ten? Remember what he was saying about what he called "sleep hygiene?" To refresh your memory, he found that the symptoms of sleep deprivation in adolescents CLOSELY MIMICKED the symptoms of ADD, ADHD and hyperactivity! You wouldn't want your child to be FALSELY DIAGNOSED (and perhaps even medicated) and stuck with one of these labels just because they've been "burning the candle at both ends" and not getting enough sleep. Kids, especially teenagers, love yaking on their cell phones, playing video games and posting on Facebook all night long, but believe me if you let them do this, the next day, academically, THEY WON'T BE GOOD FOR SHIT! You can't trust them to go to bed when they say that they are. You're the parent, you might have to go into their room at a certain hour and UNPLUG THINGS. If you don't do this, YOU MAY WELL REGRET IT!

4) MAKE SURE THAT YOUR CHILD EATS A NUTRITIOUS, BALANCED DIET, AND ONE THAT'S LOW IN SUGARY SNACKS. Any pediatrician will tell you how important good nutrition is for babies and toddlers and, despite the fact that parents tend to get lax in this regard as their kids get older, this continues to be a crucial component for our children's physical and mental health as they become big middle schoolers and teenagers as well! Again, going back to Chapter Ten, remember what we learned from the book, "Mental Health: Not all in the Mind- a Matter of Cellular Biochemistry", by Chris Melitis and Jason Barker. That book, as well as many other studies, teaches us the role adequate nutrition plays in fueling a young mind so that it's capable of properly receiving knowledge. We also saw (and I personally witnessed at Williams) how elevated sugar levels, "sugar shock" episodes where kids were bouncing off the wall, could MIMIC

ALL THE SYMPTOMS OF WHAT THE EDUCATIONAL ESTABLISHMENT CALLS "HYPERACTIVITY." Once again, you as a parent DON'T WANT YOUR CHILD TO BE MIS-DIAGNOSED, and stuck with the life-long label of being "hyperactive", when really, the only problem is an excess of sugar consumption! Check your child's book bag and see what he or she is bringing to school. And, BE AWARE OF THE FACT THAT KIDS ARE SNEAKY! I saw kids, in the morning before school at Williams, stopping at a convenience store and BUYING CANDY BARS, that they would then stuff into their book bags and sneak into class. These kids would munch on candy bars all day long and drive us staff crazy! Their parents were probably never even aware of what they were doing. So, give your child's teacher PERMISSION TO CHECK YOUR KIDS' BACKPACKS and CONFISCATE SWEETS OR CANDY BARS THAT ARE NOT SUPPOSED TO BE THERE!

5) MAKE SURE THAT YOUR CHILD GETS PLENTY OF EXERCISE. In the last chapter we saw that you can't count on your child getting the exercise that they desperately need during school hours. Most likely they've been forced to sit quietly in their seats for the six hours that they've been there, and they're going to come home full of pent-up energy. When they get home, send them OUTSIDE TO PLAY! Your kids should be jogging, swimming, playing basketball, soccer, baseball or football for at least one hour straight as SOON AS THEY GET HOME FROM SCHOOL. If, unfortunately, you live in a neighborhood where outdoor activities are unsafe, pay for your child to join a gym-and make sure that he or she goes there daily. Budget-conscious alternatives to gym membership might be a YMCA/YWCA, a community rec. hall or a Police Athletic League center or a community pool. Any place where you can make sure that your child is getting the exercise that they need for their health. Remember, a HEALTHY STUDENT IS A BETTER STUDENT!

The hour that your child is spending in healthy exercise is an hour your kid won't have to play those infernal video games that they all love to play. These violent games are a scourge upon our youth. I'm sure that their effects on our kids' minds are detrimental. The young boy, just out of his teens, named Adam Lanza, who massacred the twenty innocent first graders in Newtown-only a few miles from my home- was said to have been obsessed with these types of games. And the nine- year- old child who was recently in the news for making fools of the TSA (he snuck successfully through a major airport without going through security and managed to fly to Las Vegas without a ticket) originally came to the police's attention because he had stolen a car. When his father was asked as to why his son had stolen the car, he stated that the boy was obsessed with the video game "Grand Theft Auto" and that he wanted, in real life, to commit the crimes that he SO ENJOYED COMMITING in the video game! Do your child a favor and DON'T BUY HIM OR HER ANY OF THESE TYPES OF GAMES. If they get the games from someone or somewhere else DRASTICALLY LIMIT the amount of time that they're allowed to spend on them.

6) **IF YOUR CHILD HAS VISION PROBLEMS, HAVE THEM CORRECTED.**

According to the non-profit organization "Prevent Blindness in America" one in four school-age children have problems that, if left untreated, can affect learning ability, personality and adjustment in school. Educators have recently announced that they've found a very strong correlation between uncorrected vision difficulties in students and misbehavior and acting out episodes in school. Near-sighted kids, placed in the rear of classrooms by clueless teachers, can't follow the lessons, become bored, lose interest and become class cut-ups! Make sure that your child can easily see the blackboard (or whatever new-fangled device the teacher is now presenting the lessons on) otherwise he or she may start to fall way behind, and may NEVER CATCH UP. I saw this myself at Williams, kids sitting in the back of the classrooms, getting lost because they couldn't see, and gradually turning into class clowns or troublemakers. Don't let this happen to your kid! But again, you as a parent have to be aware of how the foolish attitudes of child-hood may be holding your son or daughter back. KIDS ARE VAIN and often don't want to wear their glasses for cosmetic reasons! They don't like the way that they look, peers can tease them, or whatever.

If you can afford to do so, get your child contact lenses; but otherwise, if they're supposed to be wearing glasses, MAKE SURE THAT THEY'RE REALLY WEARING THEM! Their glasses aren't going to be doing them any good if they're just sitting in the bottom of your child's book bag. As a para, at least five or six times a day I had to remind youngsters to put their spectacles on! The Lion's club and other worthwhile community organizations can help you get glasses for your child if you can't personally afford them yourself. If your child doesn't seem to be grasping his lessons CHECK WITH HIS TEACHER to make sure that he's wearing his glasses during class. And, oh yeah, while you're getting your kid's vision checked out; have their hearing checked too. Studies have shown that inability to hear in class is another massively underestimated cause of sub-par student performance.

7) SUPERVISE YOUR CHILD'S HOMEWORK AND SCHOOL ASSIGNMENTS. When your kid's done playing outside for an hour when they first get home from school, the time has come for you to sit down with them and supervise their homework and other school assignments. If you're a working parent and don't get home until suppertime then start this process right after supper but BEFORE THE CHILD TURNS ON THE TV OR BEGINS TO PLAY ON THE COMPUTER! Many communities (including mine) now have homework help lines where volunteer retired teachers can help the both of you if, while working on an assignment, you two get stuck. I know for a fact that the "Big Y" supermarket chain sponsors one of those services in our area. Find out about services like this where you live. You should go to your school's parent-teacher nights and speak with each of your child's teachers and find out what their expectations are regarding homework, which nights it will be assigned, and so on. In grades above elementary school, where most likely your kid's going to be having more than one teacher, you'll probably find it best to bring a little notebook along so that you can write down each of the different teachers' homework criteria. Many schools now have a parent-teacher e-mail link (my school system called it "Progress Book"), where you can log on and find out what your child's homework and other assignments are. If your school system has this, and you have access to a computer, utilize

it; otherwise call your youngster's teachers frequently to follow up on their progress. KIDS CAN BE LAZY; so at no time should you just blindly believe them when they tell you, with a straight face, "I ain't got no homework." If you're conscientious about keeping up with your child's schoolwork and assignments, you're not going to be facing any big surprises when you meet with the teachers during the four times yearly conferences. You, unlike other parents, won't ever be horrified and totally blind-sided by the words, "Your child is failing."

An interesting book on how to supervise your child, and their educational progress, is the best seller "Battle Hymn of the Tiger Mother" by Amy Chu.

Here you'll get insights into the practices of mothers who've used the traditional oriental methods so as to get the absolute best performance possible out of their children. I'm not saying, dear reader, that you necessarily want to become a "Tiger Mom" while raising your kids but, you've got to admit, that it sure beats being a disinterested absentee parent! I'm afraid to say that TOO MANY of our parents today, ESPECIALLY IN OUR INNER-CITIES, have fallen into that trap.

But one thing that I'd like to caution is that we SHOULDN'T LIVE VICARIOUSLY through our children! Let your children, without pressure from you; find their OWN ROAD and THEIR OWN happiness. Please don't say, for example, that they have to attend college just because you always thought that you should have gone there; or because it has brought success into your own life. Don't herd them into some prestigious "professional" field just so that you can brag to your friends how high up the ladder they're zooming! THEIR OWN HAPPINESS has to come from THEIR OWN INTERESTS and THEIR OWN ABILITIES- not yours. As we've said so many times before in this book, much better a happy carpenter or plumber, than an unhappy school teacher, lawyer or other society exalted "Professional!" And besides, as we've again mentioned before, if you push your child to go to college for reasons of prestige or because you want to fulfill your own frustrated destiny-and the child has no intrinsic interest in being there- they're probably just going to end up DROPPING OUT, and accomplishing nothing at all, EXCEPT LOADING THEMSELVES UP with tens of thousands of dollars of useless student loans!

8) **IF AT ALL POSSIBLE SPEAK ENGLISH AT HOME IN FRONT OF YOUR CHILD, AND LET THEM GROW UP SPEAKING ENGLISH AS THEIR PRIMARY LANGUAGE.** This is not to say that you and your family shouldn't be proud, or even celebrate your ethnic background; nor I am suggesting that your child not be taught to speak your ancestral tongue. Indeed, being bi-lingual is a GREAT ASSET in today's job market. Spanish is quickly becoming America's new second language! But be that as it may, when your son or daughter gets to school, English is the primary language that's going to be spoken there, and you don't want a language barrier causing them to fall behind in any way. The goal should be that your kid, by the time that he's ready to start school, will be FLUENT ENOUGH IN ENGLISH so that the establishment doesn't have to shunt him into the dreaded ESL (English as a Second Language) program. From what I've seen, lessons in most subjects in ESL are "dumbed down" while the teachers concentrate on trying to get the kids to read, write and speak English. This is often a massive waste of time as the children are usually much better able to speak and understand English that the educrats are willing to admit!

At Williams, for example, I often observed groups of kids in the ESL program laughing and joking in English in the back of the classroom, but when I'd correct them, they'd lapse into Spanish and pretend that they didn't understand me. As I understood a little of the language myself from my travels in Spain, I became bitterly aware of the fact that they were making fun of me and, MORE INPORTANTLY, that they were using their so-called inability to understand English as a CRUTCH and as a way to slide on out from under correction! Meanwhile, the Hispanic teacher at the front of the class was babbling on with some type of baby lesson that had everyone bored to tears. Don't let this scenario become your child's future!

9) **IF AT ALL POSSIBLE, TRY TO PREVENT YOUR CHILD FROM BEING LABELED AND "PIGEON-HOLED" BY THE EDUCATIONAL ESTABLISHMENT.** As we learned in Chapter Ten, the very existence of many of these pejorative child-classifications

(ADD, ADHD, Hyperactivity) that the educational establishment loves to throw around and use to pigeonhole kids is somewhat questionable. Even if we grant that these recently minted diagnostic jargons are of some value in describing the learning difficulties of children, we've also seen that many kids (if not the vast majority) who are platooned into these much-used categories by the schools are there as a result of MISDIAGNOSIS! What's happening here is a displacement of guilt. The educational establishment, the school, and your child's teacher, are FAILING TO CONNECT TO YOUR CHILD and, instead of owning up to their own failures, are turning the whole thing around and implying that your kid is somehow disabled. Instead of seeing the school and the teacher as a failure, it's easier for them to believe that your son or daughter is the failure. It's simply a case of BLAME THE VICTIM! In some urban districts (like mine) today up to one fourth of all the children are categorized as "special ed." What's really happening is the inability of the current school system to educate, and so as to off-load the guilt from themselves, the educrats want to see a vast number of our children as suffering from sort of a disorder. Funny, teachers and principals years ago never looked at children this way! They could play the cards as they were dealt and didn't have to blame the deck. Do these people ever bother to think about the damage that they're doing to our sons' or daughters' psyches when they pin these kinds of labels on them? Don't let them get away with it!

Was your child, when he was younger, adequately able to learn things when you taught him personally? Did he or she do well in previous school settings or with previous teachers in previous schools? Well then, the problem is probably not with your child; instead the PROBLEM IS PROBABLY WITH THE CURRENT SCHOOL OR THE CURRENT TEACHER! Stand up for your kid. Don't let them get shuffled off into one of those categories where the educrats' expectations for them will be limited, their classes will be boring, and their future will be truncated. Heck, if the educational establishment can "mainstream" the juvenile delinquents sitting beside your kid in his classroom, if they can " mainstream" the disrespectful class clowns and cut-ups in there; they should certainly be able to mainstream your child too. It's the least that you can ask!

10) **TRY TO PREVENT THE EDUCATIONAL ESTABLISHMENT- AND THEIR MEDICAL ALLIES- FROM FORCING YOUR CHILD TO TAKE BEHAVIOR ALTERING MEDICATIONS.** Again, dear reader, I urge you to go back and re-read Chapter Ten. Take a look there at the side effects drugs like Ritalin and Adderall can cause. Absorb again the reluctance of ethical doctors and researchers like Professor Szasz and Doctor Michael Andreson have in being forced to prescribe these dangerous medications to children. Does your child really need them? Is the school system zonking out your kid because it's really necessary for them to learn, or are they doing it for their own convenience instead? Schools and teachers love docile students, they make for easier teachers' days, but what about the long- range effects on your child AND THEIR HEALTH? If your child was studying what he wanted to study, and if he was interested in what he was learning at school, it probably wouldn't be necessary to put his brain into la-la land on a daily basis just to get him through the day! I've hammered again and again in this book that the school and the establishment should be there to serve your child and not the other way around. It seems to me (as well as many other researchers) that the wide spread use of these drugs is being done FOR THE CONVENIENCE OF THE STAFF and not with the child's best interests in mind. If your child's current school is trying to railroad you into putting your child on any of these types of drugs maybe you should be questioning that particular school setting. Before allowing, willy-nilly, your child to be medicated it might behoove you to look at transferring your kid into another classroom, or to another teacher, or to another more congenial, easier for your child to deal with, SCHOOL SETTING. The adult that your child is going to become some day will thank you!

11) **INSTILL GOOD VALUES IN YOUR CHILD.** Due to the chronic misunderstanding that our educational establishment has for the phrase "separation of church and state" this is one, Mister and Mrs. parent, that you're basically going to have to work on yourself. Because your kid's teacher is DEATHLY AFRAID of stepping on the toes of some splinter group or other that will object to her enlightening your child

as to the long-held moral standards of our nation's dominant Judeo-Christian culture the whole weight of this crucial job will necessarily have to fall on you. But still, come hell or high water, instilling good values into your child is something that obviously must be done. In fact, in my opinion, your child's learning good values is FAR MORE IMPORTANT than any of the purely academic information that they will ever learn, whether within, or outside of school.

And your work's cut out for you on this one! Since he or she's been born, your child has watched tens of thousands of hours of TV and movies where every single problem has been SOLVED BY VIOLENCE either in a half hour, a one hour, or a two hour format! They've grown up in a steroid sports obsessed America that sees the entire world as a Darwinian struggle for survival and mastery. A nature red in tooth and claw where winning isn't just the thing, IT'S THE ONLY THING! Aggression, stepping on rivals, pushing people out of the way is seen as how we should do things. And that goes for the girls too, being a "lady" now a days is an anachronism! Celebrities cheat, cut corners, punch people out, and get arrested but are still idolized by almost everyone. Violent video games that your kids spend hours and hours on portray a world where survival depends on killing first, and killing fast, before a quick popping up enemy can strike. It's SHOOT FIRST OR DIE- a "Hunger Games" kind of environment. Sportsmanship and fair play are considered almost as anachronistic as being a lady. Still, one should think of the fact that IF YOU RAISE YOUR CHILD AT THE BOTTOM OF A TIOLET YOU SHOULDN'T BE SURPISED IF HE GROWS UP STINKY!

We condemn bullying, but the attitudes that beget bullying are quite accepted; no maybe even celebrated, in our culture. You know the attitudes that I mean: might makes right, our "in crowd" group deserves special privileges and immunities from punishment, and that the feelings of the weak (or "losers" as we call them) are unimportant. Knowingly or not, we've taught our children that appearances are everything, and that it's OK to pass judgement on people based on superficial things like the clothes that they wear or the cars they drive. No wonder bullying has now become an epidemic in our schools and is occurring at all time record high levels! I saw it every day. Yet, this must all be turned around. And the slickly produced videos that the educrats are showing your children, with their well-paid favorite sports heroes as the narrators, aren't going to do the trick.

Where should we start? Is it hopeless? It may sound trite, but I think that it starts with you taking your child to church or synagogue. Have them make their First Holy Communion or their Bar Mitzvah. Talk to them about your own values, and your family's values going back through the generations. TEACH THEM RIGHT FROM WRONG and let them see you BEING KIND TO OTHERS and DOING GOOD WORKS. If you yourself have fallen away from religion over the years, have them speak to grandparents or others in the family who may still have some sort of a religious grounding. Because we all love them and want to see the best for our children, we're often tempted to start preaching at them. But we've got to be careful not to come off as hypocrites. If you've told your child not to smoke or do drugs, but every day he sees you puffing away and getting high, you know darned well that he's going to fluff off everything that you've said. YOU HAVE TO PRACTICE WHAT YOU PREACH. Otherwise you run the risk of losing all credibility. I can tell you with certainty that the old "Do as I say, but not as I do" type of advice IS NOT GOING TO FLY with today's kids! There are some groups like the Boy or Girl Scouts, the Police Athletic Leagues, or some well-coached sports teams that can help you instill some good old traditional values into your child that will stand them in good stead as the years go on. Don't be afraid to set down strict rules your children must follow while they're under your supervision. Back in the 60's my Dad used to say, so often that my ears got tired of hearing it, "You live under my roof, you follow my rules." He also said, "My way or the highway!" We should all be striving now to bring some of these effective parenting practices up into the 21st century. Your job, Mister and Mrs. Parent, is to be YOUR CHILD'S BEST PARENT not YOUR CHILD'S BEST FRIEND. There's a big difference.

Here in my city we had a much- respected Board of Education Commissioner named John Theriault whom I've had the great honor to have known and to have worked with. Before being elected to the Board, Mr. Theriault had been a long serving school principal and successful educator. John had an adage that he taught all the children that he ever came into contact with, it went, "IT'S NICE TO BE IMPORTANT, BUT IT'S MORE IMPORTANT TO BE NICE." If only we could get all of our children to live by-and internalize- that sentiment! Strange as it may seem, this is the one and only road that our children may use to ascend to their happiness.

Think about it dear parent, no matter how much success in life, no matter how much material wealth your child may garner, if that success is predicated on naked aggression, if that success is based on stepping on people, how much happiness can your child truly have? When your child isn't a nice person, kind to their fellow classmates and respectful to their teachers, when they have a hostile "hooray for me- to hell with everybody else" attitude, they telegraph that attitude and that hostility towards everyone surrounding them. We can turn the golden rule over upside down on its head! People will treat us in the same way that we have treated them. Sensing the self-centered, aggressive, hostile manner he's using to get over on the world, the world is going to push back at him and your child is NOT GOING TO BE LIKED by either his fellow students or his teachers. It becomes a war of "all against all" and as your child is only one, and the rest of the world are many, your child, in the long run- despite whatever early victories he might have won with his aggressive ways- MUST INEVITABLY LOSE OUT! The isolated child growing up like this, in constant conflict with his peers, and forever butting heads with his teachers and other authorities, is facing a cold and dark adulthood. The parents who have failed him in his moral education have basically drawn the blueprints for him to LIVE A LIFE OF UNENDING MISERY! Not for nothing can I say with confidence that you, as a parent, will do your child less harm if you box his ears every day the minute that he gets home from school, than you'll do IF YOU FAIL TO TEACH HIM TO LIVE BY, AND INTERNALIZE, Commissioner Theriault's happiness-birthing maxim!

12) KEEP YOUR CHILD FROM BAD COMPANY. Once you've started to get your child on the high, moral, optimistic and positive road towards a good life, the trick is to keep him or her there. What with

all of the terrible examples and influences surrounding them in today's America, this too, is going to be a tough, up-hill battle! But you can greatly improve your odds for success if you can keep your kid away from the misbehaving children whose attitudes and actions would have the effect of counteracting the good values that you've been teaching. Mankind, since time immemorial, has recognized the importance of this. For example the Good Book says, "He who touches pitch blackens his hand; he who associates with an impious man learns his ways." (Sir. 13:1). Children learn for other children and they can, unfortunately, JUST AS EASILY LEARN bad attitudes and ways of behaving as THEY CAN GOOD ONES! This is the main reason that in the next (AND LAST) section of this book we're going to be discussing- at length- YOUR CHOICE of school that you child should be attending.

I remember when I was a social worker working for the State one of my saddest jobs was to work with the families of adolescents (actually young juvenile delinquents) whose totally out-of-control behavior necessitated that the State of Connecticut place them into some sort of residential treatment center or reform school. I had extensive conferences with these heart-struck parents whose children were being sent away, and would always conduct a sort of post-mortem with them to determine exactly how it was that their children had gotten themselves onto such a road of tears. INVARIABLY and WITHOUT EXCEPTION, these crying parents all told me that their problems had begun when their child had fallen in with "THE WRONG CROWD." Now I'm not saying these parents were totally blameless in the way that they raised their children, or that they were even completely objective, BUT I AM TELLING YOU VERBATIM WHAT THEY ALL SAID! You can dismiss it if you like, but you know, if everybody unanimously says something, there's a good chance that it might be true. A word to the wise.

Get to know your child's friends, both the ones they actually see and know physically, and their cyber-friends on the internet. Heck, we've recently seen cases in Florida and in other states, where children have been arrested (and, oh yeah their parents have been hauled off with them too) for cyber-bullying so don't wait for the cops to start banging on the door before you begin supervising your son or daughter's

Facebook postings! Modern courts, whether it's fair or not, refuse to accept parents' excuses that they're ignorant about computers, or don't know about the internet. I know that it's a whole new world out there, and for us old folks it can be quite off-putting and downright scary, but for our kids' sakes we're going to have to plunge in and learn about it, no matter how difficult it may be.

I know that as children get older, especially as they reach their teen-age years, your influence with them, dear parent, starts to wane. Still, I think that you'd be surprised that when you give it your all, and really swing for the fences, your impact on them is going to be a whole lot greater than you think. If you begin to see your child starting to associate and identify with an anti-establishment, anti- school, even pre- criminal crowd; you have to start doing absolutely EVERYTHING IN YOUR POWER to nudge them away from those types of classmates! I know that we just said a few paragraphs ago that we shouldn't judge books by their covers, but I'm sure that you're aware that now- a -days, members of this poisonous clique can often be identified by their overly- abundant tattoos and body piercings. STEER YOUR KID AWAY FROM THIS GROUP! My mother (and possibly your mother as well) had a saying: "Birds of a feather flock together." Keep in mind that your child is going to have a much better- and happier- life growing up to be a DOVE instead of growing up to be a CROW! You only have ONE CHANCE to raise your child, there's no "do overs", so make your child's childhood a good one, and set them on the right and happy path.

13) EVALUATE YOUR CHILD'S SCHOOL. Let's assume that you've already done the twelve things we've recommended in this chapter and that your child is still floundering. What to do next? You're going to have to take a closer look at where your child is going to school, and determine if that school is "cutting the mustard" for the children it serves in general, and for YOUR CHILD IN PARTICULAR. Is it a failing school? How is it ranked? Is it a "drop out factory" like the failing schools we've been describing in this book, or are they doing a basically decent job of educating children there and whatever problems are occurring are, instead, specific to your child alone? These are

the questions that you should be asking, and the answers can be found easily enough (at least regarding the school's ranking) on the internet or at your local or State Board of Education's office. If, because of geographic bad luck, your kid, like Jaime's in the movie "Won't Back Down", is assigned by the educrats to a failing school, you're going to have some tough choices to make. Maybe you might want to consider home schooling your child. Possibly due to the mushrooming proliferation of failing schools, home schooling according to the "Education News" magazine, has INCREASED BY 75% during just the PAST FOURTEEN YEARS alone!

But let's get one thing straight. Just because your child gets assigned to a failing school that doesn't mean that he or she is automatically not going to get a good education. Despite everything that I've written in this book, and all the things we've talked about, I have to be truthful and vouch for the fact that some kids DID GET A VERY FINE EDUCATION AT WILLIAMS. And I'm sure that some children are getting great learning results at other failing schools throughout this great country of ours as well. Maybe your child will be lucky and get a great teacher like Ms. Stango, or maybe if you push for it, and your kid has the grades and the good behavior to qualify, they can get assigned to the "Academy" portion of the failing school (remember the "School within the school" concept that we talked about?) where he's going to get the best teachers and have only limited contact with the distracting chowder head students rampaging throughout the rest of the building. I don't know. Maybe your child is just going to work two or three times harder than everyone else does just to compensate for the headwinds he's facing; I've seen great students do that too. All I know is that you've sent your boy or girl into a race with weights chained to their feet!

But let's take a look at a worst- case scenario here. Assume that you can't get your child into the Academy portion of the school (or that it doesn't exist) and that the educrats have stuck him with the sort of clock punching, do the minimum type teachers that we've been exposing throughout this book. What then? Well, you're going to have to start making some alternative plans. You know what they say; "Those who fail to plan, plan to fail!" You can make plans to send your child to a well-run, efficient, respected religious or charter school in your city. This is most likely going to be rather expensive, as 99% of all American cities DO NOT HAVE A VOUCHER SYSTEM, so you're going to have to fund the entire expense yourself. But don't worry- YOUR CHILD IS WORTH IT! ☺

As I was writing this book, and I let out a little bit to people what it was all about, my friends told me, "Jim, you're being too hard on our inner city schools. Their problems are based on poverty, it's not their fault." In some ways, it's true, my friends do have a point; there is a direct and undeniable correlation in this country between the wealth of a city or suburb and the test scores of their children, and the percentage of their schools that are performing in the highest quartiles. But I think that POVERTY is getting a bad rap here. I don't think that it's the CASH ITSELF that's piled up in those toney suburbs that's causing the students there to score so well and their schools to be first class. After all, we had REAL POVERTY back during the Great Depression, yet America's school system; back in those days, was the envy of the world! My grandparents told me the stories of the want at that time and I'm sure that, compared to then, whatever poverty we're seeing today in 21st century America is nothing more than a walk in the park. As a matter of fact I would argue, along with many other authors and researchers, that TRUE POVERTY- you know, the kind that you might find in Haiti or sub-Saharan Africa- NO LONGER EXISTS IN THE UNITED STATES AT ALL! To quote columnist Fred Reed, "America has precious little poverty, if by poverty you mean lack of something to eat, clothing adequate to keep you warm and cover your private parts, and a dry and comfortable place to sleep. In the 'inner cities' or, as we used to call them, slums, there is a horrendous cultural emptiness, yes, and the products of the suburban high schools are catching up fast. But poverty? The kind you see in the back streets of Port-au-Prince? It barely exists in the United States."

Douglas J. Besharov, a professor at the University of Maryland School of Public Policy, averred that while "there is still some real hunger in America, it is found predominantly among people with behavioral or emotional problems, such as drug addicts and the dysfunctional homeless." Meanwhile, research by Robert Rector with the Heritage Foundation has found that 80% of households that have been designated by the government as being "poor" have air conditioning, 70% have cable or satellite TV, 60% have computers and video games and 31% own two or more cars or trucks!

So what is this "poverty" in the inner city that my friends (and everyone else) is talking about? It's a category pulled out of thin air by government bureaucrats who have created the official definition of poverty by arbitrarily designating a certain low annual income number, below which, supposedly, a family is "poor." By lumping a vast percentage of our population- an actual majority in many of our cities- into that dismal subset, they've created the rational for our current welfare state and, by the way; provided an employment industry (like teaching) for hundreds of thousands of middle class college graduates in the "helping" industries such as social work, parole and probation, counseling, etc.& etc   I probably shouldn't complain, I myself was employed in that field earlier in life. But what I find interesting, is that the income number that the poverty bureaucrats banter around, DOESN'T INCLUDE the value of the BENEFITS HANDED OUT to the "poor" such as Section 8 housing (where the recipient's monthly rent, except for a small portion, is paid for by the government), food stamps, free medical and dental (under Medicaid), transportation services and so on. WHEN THOSE BENEFITS ARE FACTORED IN it turns out that, in 35 out of 50 of our states, the "welfare poor" have it over and above the "working poor" by a long shot. Some economists have even estimated that a privately employed worker would have to earn TWENTY DOLLARS AN HOUR to replicate the lifestyle that the welfare poor enjoys without even getting out of bed.

Heck, if you can make $20 an hour forget about being "working poor", I think you could consider yourself a member in good standing of this country's dwindling middle class!

But this is not to say that there isn't a TRUE POVERTY in our blighted inner cities. It's not a poverty that has anything to do with a lack of material things, or even cash, but it's rather a poverty of ideas, a poverty of aspirations, a poverty of low expectations. It's a poverty of morals and an inability to follow the time tested and honored traditional American way of life.   It's the rise there, indeed the prevalence, of what columnists have called the hip-hop or "slob" culture (if such a back to Neanderthal lifestyle can validly be called a "culture") it's a place where 80-90% of the children come from fatherless homes and their mothers have children by three or four different men!

On the other hand, in those Toney suburbs that we spoke of, there is a TRUE WEALTH- but it's not just a wealth of cash in the bank, or McMansion houses- although those things do exist there, it's WEALTH OF HUMAN QUALITY, A WEALTH OF MORAL VALUES, THE WEALTH OF A LIFESTYLE BASED ON WORK AND STRIVING! What we generally find in these suburbs are MARRIED COUPLES, usually dual earner families (often with substantial incomes), raising their children in the old fashioned, American tried and true way. Statistics show that poverty is very, very rare in this country among MARRIED COUPLES. So we probably shouldn't really be surprised that there's substantial financial wealth out there too! But that's not the point. It's the moral example of the intact family homes, with their emphasis on hard work and striving, that gives their children a MIGHTY BOOST up the ladder to success.

Comparing the culture and lifestyle of the middle class suburb to the lifestyle and "culture" of the pathological inner city regarding school performance columnist George Will describes it this way: " Abundant data demonstrate the vast majority of differences in schools' performances can be explained BY QUALITIES OF THE FAMILIES from which the children come to school. The amount of homework done at home, the quantity and quality of reading material in the home, the amount of television watched in the home and, much the most important variable, THE NUMBER OF PARENTS in the home. In Chicago, 84% of African-American children and 57% of Hispanic children are born to unmarried women. The city is experiencing an epidemic of youth violence- a 38% surge in the homicide rate, 53 people shot on a recent weekend, and random attacks by roving youth mobs. Social regression, driven by family disintegration, means schools where teaching is necessarily subordinated to the arduous task of maintaining minimal order." Which is EXACTLY WHAT I WITNESSED at Williams!

To take a look at just how far this downward spiraling horror of inner city pathology can go, one need only take a look at the City of Detroit. In 1950 Detroit was the fifth largest city in the nation with a population of 1,850,000. Today, less than 713,000 people live there, almost anyone who possibly can has moved out! Why did so many people move out of Detroit? The quick answer: crime abetted by welfare. During the decade from 1965 to 1975, crime and welfare dependency quadrupled in Detroit. There was a connection between the two trends. Welfare encouraged single parenthood; and fatherless boys often grew up to commit violent crimes. The results? Today dangerous packs of feral dogs rampage through forgotten urban wastelands. Many of Detroit's residents are now functionally illiterate, only 12% have a college degree and 80% of the children are born to unwed mothers. Think about it, what middle class family in their right mind would entrust their children to a public school system where only 3% of the fourth graders meet national math standards? Things have gotten so bad there that Rick Synder, Michigan's new governor, is bulldozing enormous swathes of land where abandoned homes, factories and warehouses once stood, and replanting these areas with miles of trees, parks and open land. Heck, maybe the folks left behind can GO BACK TO FARMING or HUNTING FOR FOOD!

Lord knows that there's got to be plenty of room for parks, trees and open space now that the city has 78,000 abandoned structures!

And how are our black children doing in this whirlwind of destruction that the liberals have brought us with President Lyndon Johnson's (who by the way I admired) "Great Society?" Let's let black columnist Walter Williams speak on that one. He wrote, "The educational system, and black family structure and culture, have combined to make increasing numbers of young black people virtually useless in the increasingly high-tech world of the 21st century. Too many people believe pouring more money into schools will help. That's whistlin' 'Dixie'. Whatever a student's racial or economic background, there are some minimum requirements that must be met in order to do well in school.

SOMEONE MUST MAKE THE STUDENT DO HIS HOMEWORK, see to it that he gets a good night's sleep, fix a breakfast, make sure he gets to school on time, and make sure he respects and obeys his teachers. Here are my questions: Which one of those requirements can be achieved through a higher school budget? Which can be achieved by politicians? If those minimal requirements aren't met, whatever else is done IS MOSTLY FOR NAUGHT." I'd suppose that if you wanted to take a chance that your son was going to become a hip-hop star like Eminem (who, by the way does hail from Detroit), or a basketball star in the NBA, your might want to stick with an inner city school system of the type that we've been describing, but if you're doing some sort of rational assessment of your child's future, probably not!

I would like to apologize friend reader for the dark and gloomy, some might even say mean-spirited, tenor that this narrative has taken on in the last few pages. Anyone who knows me though, I'm sure would tell you that I'm a very good-hearted, warm, giving and loving person. During the years I worked at Williams, no matter how outrageous the kids' antics were, or how blatant their disrespect was, my heart went out to them and I tried to help them to the very best of my ability. That's because I fully understood the horrible backgrounds that they were coming from, and I felt SORRY FOR THEM. I consider myself to be a good Christian and, in fact, am a lector for my church on Sundays. I mention all this as a preface to, what I am sure will be considered to be, the extremely politically incorrect statements that I'm going to be forced to make in the last few pages of this book. I'll be making these statements, not out of any kind of malice for or hard-heartedness to, the TRULY DISADVANTAGED AMONG US but rather in my attempt to HELP YOUR CHILD; which indeed has been the whole rationale behind this work from the beginning!

We have to start with an objective, dispassionate look at the people left behind in the dwindling populations of our crime-ridden, blighted, violence prone inner cities; let's go ahead and call them slums for that is what they truly are. Few of these places (and certainly not my city) have regressed into the hellish holocaust that Detroit has, but from Detroit we can get an idea of where they're heading and what the trends are. So who are these people, and what are they like? You know, the denizens of the ghetto who are going to be sending their kids to fill up the classrooms sitting side by side with your child in these failing inner city schools?

Of course we must start with the ubiquitous unwed mother, the center of the whole thing that we've spoken about ad nauseam throughout this book. This woman, the titular head of her fragmented family, frequently has three or more children by just as many fathers. She and her brood (when they're not homeless or wandering about) live on welfare and food stamps while residing in generally run-down section 8 housing in the most dangerous parts of the city. More than likely, she's a high school dropout herself and may very well be functionally illiterate- so much for helping her kids with their homework! As she's on welfare, she doesn't have to work, SO SHE CERTAINLY CAN'T TEACH HER CHILDREN ANY KIND OF A WORK ETHIC, and being that she doesn't have to get up in the morning you can forget about her fixing her kids any kind of a breakfast. As I've spoken about at Williams, it's not at all unusual for her to be out partying all night long, so she's not going to be taking any early morning 'phone calls from the school.

And how about the men in the "Hood?" Just as they rotate incessantly in and out of "Big Mama's" house, a large percentage of them rotate in and out of our prison systems as well! Most of them "get by" somehow, criminal enterprises aren't uncommon, they work under the table and if a kid gets real lucky, maybe he'll get a dad who's holding down a minimum wage job. Many times multiple men show up at the tenement around the first of the month to vie for Big Mama's affections (and her newly received welfare check!). Unfortunately, alcoholism, drug addiction, and mental illnesses are statistically found in these populations-both the men and the women- in staggeringly greater percentages than they're found throughout the rest of society.

I know these people. For four years I was a social worker making home visits into the most blighted, troubled parts of our city. I've spent hours and hours with them in their homes. Do you want, dear reader, to know how they spend their time? Drinking (even early in the morning), drugging, playing cards, sleeping late, watching TV, ignoring the dishes and the cockroaches, while laughing their days away. Not a care in the world! Oftentimes when I made my home visits (I was trying to assess if these were suitable homes for children) I'd catch them stuffing days worth of dirty dishes, or unwashed laundry, into their seldom used ovens or cramming them into way back hall closets. They made every attempt to "get over" on me. But they could turn violent too, at the drop of a hat! If I said one thing wrong, or anything that they perceived as threatening, they'd spring up from the table, and I often had to call for police backup.

And what are the attitudes of such fine folk? Well, for one, they hate the police, teachers, the establishment, and all other forms of authority. They often don't want to work (in all honesty for many of them it wouldn't make economic sense) and can't understand why the larger world around them won't just let them drink, do drugs, and party without giving them a hard time and a lot of boring lectures!

The parenting skills of these types of people leave much to be desired; after all, if they're unable to discipline themselves they certainly aren't going to be able to discipline their children either. By and large, the progeny of these tattooed, violent, gap-toothed neer-do-wells DO NOT MAKE GOOD STUDENTS!

When you place your child into a school where most of the classrooms are going to be filled with such galoots, you have at the very least, placed your son or your daughter into a situation whereby they're going to have to work a HUNDRED TIMES HARDER just to learn as well as they would have in a more congenial setting. It's patently obvious that you should get your child out of that type of environment! Now I know that the liberals who've been reading these past few pages, especially public school teachers, CONSIDER ALL OF THIS ANATHEMA AND HAVE STEAM COMING OUT OF THEIR EARS ABOUT NOW AS THEY'RE READING THIS. They'd probably tell you that the advice that I'm offering is nothing other than the worst kind of snobbery. But these people, certainly the teachers, are nothing less than the worst kind of hypocrites. We could even describe them, as being what Jesus would call, "Whited Sepulchers!" These highly educated individuals are certainly well aware of the existence of what psychologists call "behavioral contagion." This psychological concept, which was first written about back in 1895 by Gustave Le Bon, and which has been validated by hundreds of studies, explains that behaviors (surprise! surprise!), whether GOOD or BAD, are profoundly influenced by the GROUPS with which the individual is associating.

They're also aware, I'm sure, that every SELF HELP book ever published in the last fifty years has stressed the importance of associating with POSITIVE PEOPLE, and how very crucial it is to stay away from negative influences. Wouldn't advice that's been written for adults also be applicable for our children as well? Of course the educrats know all this stuff, they know that bad behavior rubs off and can almost be CONTAGIOUS, which is why they've created the Academies- the schools within the schools- in our failing establishments so they can keep THE GOOD KIDS AWAY FROM THE BAD KIDS AND THEIR NEGATIVE INFLUENCES. It's also why public school teachers, more than any other group, are the most likely to pull their own children out of our failing inner city schools and to place them in private schools instead. Yet they're quick to tell you, dear reader, that you should go ahead and feel perfectly OK about sending your kid into that maelstrom. You know what I say? DO AS THEY PRACTICE, NOT AS THEY PREACH, follow their example and get your own children OUT OF THOSE KINDS OF PLACES! Heck, what with all of the violence happening on an almost epidemic basis in some of these schools, your child might not even be physically safe there.

Think of it this way. If your child became physically ill and had to go to a hospital, would you let some bureaucrat there send him to a contagious leprosy ward? Say they told you that the hospital was short on beds. Would that make it all right? Hell no! Would you depend on just luck that your boy or girl might come out of that contagious ward without catching leprosy? So why then would you let some educrat in your city's downtown educational department's home office assign your child to some hellhole of a school just because your house happens to be within the borders of some arbitrary geographical district? Especially when you're aware now, that the long-term deleterious effects for him in getting stuck there can easily rival the dangers of his passing his days on a leprosy ward! Of course you're going to get your kid out of a school like that!

I've sometimes said that LUCK IS THE RELIGION OF THE LAZY; but if there's anything that I'm sure of it's that you, friend reader, are not one of the lazy ones. After all, you've stuck with me through thick and thin throughout this long work, so I know that you have the wherewithal when pushed, to commence some dramatic action when IT COMES TO SAVING YOUR CHILD.

My final advice to you, if your child is continuing to struggle, and you are starting to have some doubts as to the caliber of his school, is to begin a series of on site visits. Sit in your child's classrooms with him or her, and if you observe that many, many of the children in those rooms show every appearance of being the back talking, wisecracking, tattooed, body-pierced slobs that anyone at all can legitimately identify as being the SPAWN OF THE GHETTO, then the time has come to SWOOP DOWN LIKE AN EAGLE, scoop your child up in your talons, and get them OUT OF THAT FAILING INNER CITY SCHOOL as fast as you damned can!

Get that second (or third) job and start making plans to move out of that drive-by shooting shitty (oops, I meant to say city!) and relocate out to a suburb with a good school system where your son or daughter can get a decent education. You're going to have to do a little research, as not all suburbs (especially those immediately adjacent to our major metropolitan areas) automatically have well regarded educational systems, but I'm sure that with a little effort on-line you'll be able to find one. Like I mentioned before, you're not going to get any "do-overs" regarding your child's ONE TIME childhood, so it's better to ere on the side of caution, than to take you, and your child's chances inside our increasingly violent urban wasteland areas.

Move out to where your child can breathe some crisp fresh air and run around barefoot on some nice, clean green grass. A place where you and your child can live, learn and play, and grow each day in safety and in happiness. Let it be a place where that when your child grows up and remembers his childhood, it will bring a smile to his face INSTEAD OF bitter tears. I WISH I HAD.

MOVE TO THE SUBURBS

>Move to the suburbs
>Young man.
>Grass needs sun to grow;
>Just so-
>Your son needs grass to grow! ☺

Epilogue

As the 2012 academic year began at Williams I was filled, just as I was before each and every other year and semester, with trepidation and anxiety as to what my new assignments would be. I wondered just how my luck would hold out, and exactly which teachers, classes and students that I'd draw. Fortunately, I picked up a pretty good roster. As a matter of fact, this is was when I had the great honor of being assigned to Ms. Stango's class! Sadly enough though, THERE WAS A FLY IN THE OINTMENT. As dumb luck would have it, I got assigned to work with a young science teacher who was, just that year, transferring into our school. We'll call her "Mrs. Furious." This young lady, for reasons that still to this day elude me, right from the start, made it absolutely clear that she didn't like me at all. I don't know why. In Mrs. Furious' defense, I can categorically state that by the end of the school year she had proven both to me, and to everyone else on the staff, that she was a thoroughly competent and effective teacher. Maybe she was angry that it took me so long to remember the names of all the kids in her classroom. I don't know.

Anyways, from day one in her room, there were constant problems. First of all, unlike the other teachers, she insisted that I remain totally silent in her class. Closed tight and shut away was the vast treasury of knowledge that I had gained from living on this planet for the past sixty years, that the other teachers were kind enough to let me share with the other kids in their classes! Secondly, again unlike the other teachers, she demanded that I remain standing throughout the entire forty-five minute class period, without ever sitting down once. Basically, what she wanted me to do was to stomp around the room and silently (almost threateningly) lour over the children like some kind of scary Frankenstein monster. Maybe she thought that this way I could scare them into learning better like some sort of ghoulish Halloween scarecrow!

Although I vehemently disagreed with the role (actually it might be better to say the lack of a role) that Mrs. Furious relegated me to, I followed her directions slavishly and without complaint. I did so because it was my philosophy when I was working at Williams, that I WAS JUST A PARAPROFESSIONAL, and that I was only there to take direction and guidance from whoever the certified teacher was that had been assigned to run the class. I saw myself as the teacher's helper and I thought that it was my job to assist her in whatever way she thought best. In my mind the teacher was my "boss" and I, basically, was her employee. I admit that this was sometimes a little difficult as almost all of the teachers (including Mrs. Furious) were younger than my own adult children! Still, I did my utmost to knuckle under quietly and obey.

Nevertheless, I certainly wasn't happy with the way I was being treated, and there was undoubtedly a tenseness in the classroom that must have been almost palpable. Surely, the children picked up on it. They'd often pull me aside in the hallway and ask, "Mr. Shine, Mrs. Furious doesn't like you- does she?" When they said that I'd try to pooh-pooh it, and tell them that I and Mrs. Furious were good colleagues, and that I considered her to be a good teacher and so on, but I could tell by their smirky faces that they weren't buying it!

Anyways, Mrs. Furious and I managed to limp along until the third week of the school year without any sort of major incident. But one bright September morn, while she was teaching the kids about the derivation of scientific terms, SHE DROPPED A BOMBSHELL! Mrs. Furious calmly explained to the children that many scientific terms came from Greek, because they had originally been given these names by the ancient ROMANS WHO SPOKE GREEK! You could have knocked me over with a feather! Naturally, I didn't want to undercut my teacher in front of her students, so I bit my tongue, but right after class I ran to catch up with her by the classroom door.

As politely and diplomatically as I could, I explained to her that the ancient ROMANS HAD SPOKEN LATIN, and that the reason that some of these terms had come from Greek, was that the Greeks themselves had studied many of these disciplines BEFORE THE ROMANS DID and that THE GREEKS THEMSELVES had given the terms their original names. You'd have thought that I'd smacked her across the face with a heavy pair of wet, smelly socks! Mrs. Furious crinkled up her nose, began stuttering and muttering as spittle formed at the corners of her mouth, while thunderbolts rocketed from her eyes. The laser-like glare she shot me could have melted titanium! As quick as you could say "Jack Robinson" she spun around on her heel and stalked away, all the while mumbling angrily but incoherently to herself. I could almost see trumpets of steam jetting forth at a forty-five degree angle from her ears. "I've torn it good this time," I said to myself. NOW I'M IN BIG TROUBLE!!

Sure enough, that very afternoon, she shot off a two-page e-mail to our house principal, Mr. Yesheva, demanding that I be immediately pulled out of her class, and even questioned whether I was qualified to work as a para in any sort of capacity at the school at all. Later she talked to me on the side, and suggested that I might do better working as a greeter at Walmart!

The kindly Mr. Yesheva brought both of us into his office and we had a couple of conferences where he tried to mend fences, but I think that any rational soul could clearly see that the two of us weren't meant to work together. But I was surprised to find, that due to the Byzantine bureaucracy at Williams, Mr. Yesheva, despite the fact that he was the house principal, didn't have the power to extricate me from that difficult woman's classroom. NOW I REALLY GOT SCARED! The fear that I was going to get stuck, and would have to spend the entire rest of the school year, in that hostile harpy's miniature kingdom terrified me. Looking forward to the remaining eight months, it all loomed ahead of me as if I was going to have to go the dentist for a never-ending root canal!

Luckily, I had a friend, actually my BEST FRIEND among my fellow paras, a pleasant Hispanic gentleman named Oscar, who at my request, agreed to switch classes with me. Thanks to him, I was able to get out of that strident teacher's miserable room! Because of this I shall always be eternally grateful to Mr. P., who is, by the way, a pretty darn good para himself.

The rest of the academic year passed by quite uneventfully. As a matter of fact, in many ways it was a good year, as I was assigned to Ms. Stango's class, and from her I was able to learn just how much a great teacher can accomplish- even if she's saddled with the sort of dysfunctional student population that we had to work with at Williams. But the incident with Mrs. Furious had left a bad taste in my mouth. I thought to myself, "Heck, I've got to take all of this guff and disrespect from the students, and now I've got to start taking flack from some of the teachers too?!" I began to think that life was getting to be way too short, and I was getting to be way too old, to have to go through this type of crap. I decided that once the current school year was over, that I should put in my papers, start collecting my social security, go home and retire to write my memoirs. THE MEMOIRS you're holding in your hands right now! So that's exactly what I did.

I hope these pages have brought you a few really good laughs, many more smiles, and an awful lot to think about. I'D BE SHOCKED AND AMAZED if you, dear reader, considering the controversial nature of all that I've written, AGREED COMPLETELY with everything that I've said. But still, I know that I've given you some good pointers to consider for your child as he or she wends their way through our country's faulty educational system. I've also, I'm sure, presented you with many goals and objectives for educational change that you can pursue with your own local board of education. Ideas that I beg you to push forward if you decide to become- what this country needs now most of all - a FEARLESS EDUCATIONAL REFORMER!

As I conclude I find myself feeling a kind of sadness, a sort of wistfulness, as my mind floats into a reverie imagining how THINGS MIGHT HAVE BEEN, HOW THINGS COULD HAVE BEEN, if only I had lived in a different time, or had worked UNDER A DIFFERENT SYSTEM. It all brings to my mind an ancient morality story that I read long ago that went:

"Once upon a time in ancient China there lived a little boy who was an orphan. He was being raised by his elderly grandfather and they lived in an isolated cabin in the deep woods. His grandfather had been a famous martial artist and swordsman when he was young, and to keep in shape every day, he practiced his sword-swinging passes and moves vigorously so as to keep in shape. The young boy watched him closely and attentively, but grandfather never let the youth touch the sword himself.

One day while the young man (who had now become a teenager) was away from the cabin gathering berries, brigands came and hit the grandfather on the head, and knocked him out. When the youth looked in the window he could see that the bandits were stealing every single thing that the small family had.

Bursting into the room the young one seized his grandfather's sword hanging above the fireplace and, without thinking at all, easily bested those clumsy fools and drove them into frantic flight!

And, so we learn, that showing our children something often enough, and showing them the way that they should go, can have sometimes have very good results-even if we don't realize that we are teaching!"

Yes, indeed there's no LIMIT as to what we can teach our kids, if we teach them by example and not just spend our time BLOVIATING at them. As Saint Francis of Assisi taught us SO CORRECTLY seven hundred years ago when he said, "Preach the Gospel every day, if necessary, USE WORDS."

THE END ☺

Made in the USA
Columbia, SC
04 August 2017